Mixed-Breed Dogs

LEXIANN GRANT

ANIMAL PLANET ♥ PET CARE LIBRARY

Mixed-Breed Dogs

Project Team
Editor: Mary Grangeia
Indexer: Elizabeth Walker
Design Concept: Leah Lococo Ltd., Stephanie Krautheim
Design Layout: Patricia Escabi

T.F.H. Publications
President/CEO: Glen S. Axelrod
Executive Vice President: Mark E. Johnson
Publisher: Christopher T. Reggio
Production Manager: Kathy Bontz

T.F.H. Publications, Inc.
One TFH Plaza
Third and Union Avenues
Neptune City, NJ 07753

Discovery Communications, Inc. Book Development Team
Marjorie Kaplan, President and General Manager, Animal Planet Media
Kelly Day, EVP & COO, Digital Media & Commerce
Elizabeth Bakacs, VP, Licensing & Creative
JP Stoops, Director, Licensing
Bridget Stoyko, Designer

Printed and bound in China.
10 11 12 13 14   1 3 5 7 9 8 6 4 2

Library of Congress Cataloging-in-Publication Data
Grant, Lexiann.
  Mixed-breed dogs / Lexiann Grant.
      p. cm. -- (Animal planet pet care library)
  Includes index.
  ISBN 978-0-7938-3707-6 (alk. paper)
  1. Mutts (Dogs) I. Title.
  SF427.G746 2010
  636.7--dc22

                              2009051740

This book has been published with the intent to provide accurate and authoritative information in regard to the subject matter within. While every reasonable precaution has been taken in preparation of this book, the author and publisher expressly disclaim responsibility for any errors, omissions, or adverse effects arising from the use or application of the information contained herein. The techniques and suggestions are used at the reader's discretion and are not to be considered a substitute for veterinary care. If you suspect a medical problem consult your veterinarian.

Note: In the interest of concise writing, "he" is used when referring to puppies and dogs unless the text is specifically referring to females or males. "She" is used when referring to people. However, the information contained herein is equally applicable to both sexes.

The Leader in Responsible Animal Care for Over 50 Years!®
www.tfh.com

Table of Contents

Chapter 1

Why I Adore My

Mixed-Breed Dog

quod•li•bet: *A whimsical combination of two or more; from ancient words meaning "who it pleases" and "to love."*

None other like him, the only one, the mutt is beyond comparison in looks and character. He's a special dog of a lifetime—a "quodlibet" just for you—and there will never be another that can replace him.

Mix. Mutt. Heinz 57. All-American dog. All names for dogs of uncertain parentage. Although some terms for mixed-breed dogs (mixes) are derogatory, such as cur or mongrel, most owners love their mixes as passionately as owners of purebreds love their dogs.

The terminology applied to dogs of mixed ancestry varies. Mixed breed implies a dog with at least two, but probably more, types of breeds or mixes in his background. Crossbreeds are dogs born from purebred parents of two different breeds. A hybrid is the offspring of a dog and an animal of another species, like a wolf.

Many mixes are born because owners of the parent dogs aren't responsible, letting them run loose and not spaying or neutering them. Crossbreeds may be "purpose-bred" to create a "unique" dog. And sometimes, accidents happen and there are mixed, random-bred puppies.

However you get your mix, it probably doesn't matter—you love him and see him as the world's cutest dog. But understanding a bit of his possible heritage may help you to better understand him, train him, and live with him for his lifetime.

History of the Mixed-Breed Dog

The history of mixed-breeds is the history of the dog. When dogs and humans first began their journey together, there were no Poodles or Pugs, only wolf-like canids. Climate was the biggest factor affecting a dog's appearance. Where it was cold, his fur became thick or shaggy; in hot regions, he developed a short, thin coat.

Humans paired with dogs to work, using some to hunt or herd, others to guard or move heavy loads. Over the centuries, two dogs that were good at a certain task were bred to each other to create more dogs who excelled at the same job.

A mixed-breed dog has at least two, but probably more, types of breeds or mixes in his background.

Breeds as we recognize them today didn't exist until the late 1800s. They were created in the same way as early types, but with a specific definition of breed function and physical appearance. In a sense, until recent history all dogs could be considered mixed breeds.

Today, the mutt endures and remains in all his infinite forms.

Physical and Behavioral Characteristics

There is no animal more genetically "flexible" than the dog. Dogs show more variety in size, color, shape, and fur than any other species. Types and breeds of dogs have come and gone, evolving with each generation. There are more than 400 recognized breeds, and almost as many crossbreeds.

With this many types of dogs, the possible combinations of mixed breeds are endless. A mix can be any color, build, or size. Behavior and personality can be as varied as there are different types of dogs or mixes: innumerable.

Whatever your mix looks or acts like, he is unique. Even from the same litter, no two pups are the same. But all dogs do share common traits. And even mixes may resemble one predominant type.

Northern Breeds

Northern breeds include the Siberian Husky, American Eskimo, and Pomeranian.

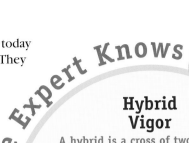

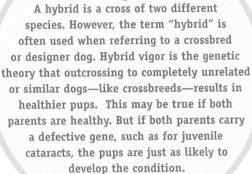

The Expert Knows

Hybrid Vigor

A hybrid is a cross of two different species. However, the term "hybrid" is often used when referring to a crossbred or designer dog. Hybrid vigor is the genetic theory that outcrossing to completely unrelated or similar dogs—like crossbreeds—results in healthier pups. This may be true if both parents are healthy. But if both parents carry a defective gene, such as for juvenile cataracts, the pups are just as likely to develop the condition.

Also known as Nordic or Spitz breeds, these dogs developed around and south of the Arctic Circle and in the high mountains of northern Asia. Their fur is thick and double-coated to keep out cold and damp, their tails curl over the back, which keeps them out of snow, and their ears are erect and heavily furred. Northern breeds are often white or shades of gray, but can be tan or red. They are heavy boned and strongly muscled, with medium length, pointed muzzles.

Northern types are highly intelligent and independent but loyal and sociable by nature. Housetraining is usually easy, but obedience training requires methods that keep the dog's interest. They need plenty of exercise or a "job" to keep them happy. Northern breeds have worked as sledding, hunting, or companion dogs, and they are seen in the hound, working, and even toy groups.

Herding Breeds

Herding breeds include Shetland Sheepdogs, Border Collies, and German Shepherd Dogs.

A hunting technique of ancient northern wolves and their canine descendants is to circle and isolate their prey. Shepherds selected northern dogs that exhibited this trait and used it to help move their flocks and herds. Herding dogs are built for agility, usually long in the middle, with proportionately sized legs and necks. Cattle herders (Corgis) have shorter legs to prevent being kicked. Their fur can be double-coated or medium in length. Tails, if present, are usually short. Herders derived from mastiff/flock guardian dogs are shaggy, with drop ears. Ears are mostly erect, but some fold, and muzzles are long. Colors are blended shades of gray, tan, black, or white.

Herders are highly-intelligent, high-energy dogs. To occupy their busy minds and bodies, they need training and exercise, as well as an owner who is active.

Mastiff Breeds

Mastiff breeds include the Rottweiler, Boxer, and Newfoundland.

Dogs show more variety in size, color, shape, and fur than any other species.

Also known as Molossers in ancient times, these dogs developed in the mountains of southern Asia. Although originally lighter bodied, as these dogs performed tasks that required strength, their large heads, short muzzles, and heavy bodies became more pronounced. Many of these dogs became short-furred as they moved into warmer climates. Colors vary, ranging from black, dark shades of gray or brown, to tans.

Ancient mastiffs were fierce in character. Today, although keen and alert, they can be stubborn but are adept pupils. Their original tasks were to serve as guards and "beasts of war," then later as cattle drovers and butchers' dogs. Modern domestic mastiffs still need a job. Steady exercise is best, as is an owner who can be a leader to these dominant dogs.

Serving as family guardians and rescue dogs, today's mastiffs mostly comprise the Working Group. Though most are large, some have been bred down to smaller sizes and are recognizable by their stout heads and bodies, and short muzzles.

Flock Guardians

Examples of flock guardians include the Great Pyrenees, Kuvasz, and Anatolian Shepherd.

Flock guardian dogs probably developed from mastiffs because of their similar build and personality, and because they originated in the same regions. As these dogs spread into the European mountains, they grew heavy, thick coats. Flock guardians today are

FAMILY-FRIENDLY TIP

Mixed Breeds and Kids

Whether your mixed-breed dog and young children will be a good match depends on how you teach them to treat your dog and the size and personality of your mix. Small, nervous, fearful, or hyper mixes are best left to adult-only households, as may be large, dominant dogs from guardian or mastiff type breeds. Calm-mannered but energetic mixes of medium size may make excellent companions for a child. Whatever the combination, always supervise children and dogs whenever they're together.

heavily built with large bones, small droop ears and low, long tails. Many of them are white or light in color, a trait that allows them to blend in with the flocks they guard.

These dogs tend to be aloof and independent, but fiercely protective. They learn quickly and are considered to be "thinkers." A job and long walks are good for flock guardians.

"Bully" Breeds

Examples of bully breeds include American Pit Bull Terriers, Bulldogs, and Bull Terriers.

A smaller mastiff type, these dogs are shorter in height but as heavily built, with large bones and strong muscles. Ears are upright, fold, or drop. Tails, when present, are thick and slightly shortened. Many of these dogs are multicolored, in shades of tan or white.

Because the bully breeds were originally fighters, their natures can be aggressive. But properly trained, they are loyal, fun-loving companions. Owners need to understand dog behavior and learn techniques for teaching these strong-willed types. These surprisingly active dogs need regular exercise.

Scenthounds

Many scenthounds were developed in western Europe, and examples include Basset Hounds, Dachshunds, and Bloodhounds.

They are another group of dogs likely descended from mastiffs—hunting dogs that use their noses to find and follow prey. Mostly short-coated, these dogs have large, droopy ears. Scenthounds come in a variety of solid or multicolors and can be distinctly marked with tri-color spots, saddles, and ear flaps. From short (Beagle) to tall (Coonhound), these dogs have broad or boxy, prominent snouts.

Scenthounds are energetic, persistent, and curious. They like to play and work but can be difficult to train.

Sighthounds

Well-known sighthounds include the Greyhound and Afghan Hound.

Although a distinct type of dog, sighthounds may also have originated from the mastiff. These dogs have exceptionally keen eyesight and a strong drive to chase prey. Sighthounds are recognizable by their long, narrow muzzles and intense gaze. They have large chests, with small waists and long legs. Their build is slender and agile, and small (Whippet) to tall (Irish Wolfhound). Most have delicate droop ears and long, gracefully curving tails. Fur can be short or long, with any variety of solid or mixed colors from whites and tans to dark grays.

Except for their brief episodes of explosive chases, sighthounds are usually couch potatoes. Exercise should be short but intense. A securely fenced area would provide an ideal space for them to run.

Sighthounds are dignified and somewhat aloof, but they love their families. They don't care what people think of them and are not easily trained. Though intelligent, they like to pretend otherwise.

Terrier type dogs tend to be very active.

Sporting Dogs

Sporting breeds include the Golden Retriever, Cocker Spaniel, and Labrador Retriever.

Also known as hunting or gun dogs, sporting breeds probably originate from mastiffs and hounds. Many types of dogs were used to create this group. Muzzles are well developed and boxy. Ears are drop and prominent. Tails are large for visibility. Build and size are dependent on the terrain and type of prey hunted, although sporting dogs tend to be stocky. Fur can be short, wavy, wiry, or curled and comes in tans, reds, blacks, whites, and combinations.

Eager to please, sporting dogs are easily trained. They are sociable companions that love to love and be loved. They also love to be busy, busy, busy, so give them the exercise they crave.

Terriers

Terrier breeds include the Scottish, Fox, and Norfolk Terriers, as well as Miniature Schnauzers.

Terrier types were found in the ancient world and later developed in the United Kingdom. It's uncertain whether they originated from mastiffs or northern dogs, or a combination of those types.

Mostly small in size with only a few exceptions, terriers were designed to catch destructive vermin. Compact but muscular, they are square built or long bodied. Ears are compact and upright, as are the shortened tails. Eyes are dark and deep-set to protect them, and a

SENIOR DOG TIP

When Is a Mix a Senior?

The age at which your mix is considered a senior depends on his size, health, and genetics. Small dogs live longer than large ones, aging gracefully until at least nine years or older. Giant dogs may be seniors as early as six years of age. In general, the average age for being a senior is seven, but with regular health care, exercise, and good nutrition, the effects of aging may come much later.

Signs of aging include:
- arthritis or joint stiffness
- circulatory problems
- decreased kidney function
- dental problems
- ear infections
- graying muzzle
- lower energy level and fatigue
- vision or hearing loss
- skin or fleshy tumors
- weight loss or weight gain

Watch your mix for these changes, and talk to your vet about how to handle the special needs of your senior so you can offer him the best quality of life possible.

wiry coat protects the body. Terriers developed in other parts of Europe have mostly short coats. They are typically, gray, tan, or cream.

Best described as temperamental, terriers may not like other animals. They want to be admired and obeyed. Although strong willed, they are very intelligent and learn quickly. Extremely active, a terrier is happiest when he's working or getting vigorous recreation.

Toys

Popular toy breeds include the Bichon Frise, Yorkshire Terrier, and Chihuahua.

Teeny companions, toy dogs are the miniatures of the canine world. Other than size, there is nothing small about them: Toys are all dog. Even though they weren't kept as working dogs, toys have existed as long as their larger counterparts.

Because they were developed from all the original group types, there is no common denominator in their appearance. Toys from Asia have flattened (brachycephalic) faces (Pug); from western Europe, long hair or elaborate fringing (Papillon); and from the Mediterranean, long white fur, floppy ears, and dark noses (Maltese). Tails are short or curled, ears drop or stand erect, fur is long, curly, short, or barely there (Chinese Crested). Colors can be anything from tan and red to black, but many toys are white or parti-colored (King Charles Cavalier Spaniel).

Toys thrive on attention and are lost without affection. They love to please and are easily trained, although

Outcrosses have been made in nearly all modern-day breeds. This Labradoodle is a cross between a Labrador and a Poodle.

housetraining is difficult and time consuming. Despite their size, their energy is high and they need lots of exercise. Because they're small, a little walking and play go a long way.

Designer Dogs

Examples of designer dogs include Cockapoos, Labradoodles, and Puggles.

The term "designer dog" is a fancy phrase for a crossbred mix. Designer dogs have been intentionally created to meet the demand of consumers looking for a status symbol pet, or a cross that is supposedly hypoallergenic or healthier than a purebred dog.

A designer mix may come from someone who has carefully chosen the parents to breed a healthy line of dogs, or he may come from a puppy mill crossbred by someone with no regard for the animals' health trying to make a quick dollar. These dogs come with exceptionally high price tags and usually have no background health checks or guarantees. Looks vary from one litter—or puppy—to another, and temperament, even if based on the parent breeds, is also unpredictable.

If you like the idea of a specific mix of two breeds, try searching for your dream combination with a purebred rescue group that places mixes of their breed. But if you have your heart set on a designer cross, locate a breeder who cares more about the health and welfare of the dogs than about the prices they command.

Famous Mixes

Famous Owners

Balto: Husky/wolf hybrid who led the last sled team that delivered antitoxin serum for a diphtheria epidemic in Nome, Alaska in 1925

Benji: Real-life dog actors Higgins, Benji #2, and Benji #3 starred in the movie Benji and its sequels about a lovable mutt adopted from a shelter who somehow manages to help people overcome their problems

Murray: TV funny dog actor Maui, who was originally found in a shelter by his trainer, played the dim-witted but lovable border collie mix in the Mad About You series

Laika: Real-life Soviet space dog, a Samoyed/Husky mix, who was the first animal to orbit the earth

Tiger: TV dog actor Tiger played the shaggy family dog in the Brady Bunch series

Velvet: Real-life adopted black Lab mix who helped keep three stranded hikers on Mt. Hood warm and alive until their rescue

Alicia Silverstone: Rescue dogs Samson (Rottweiler/Pit Bull mix), Cale, Scottie, Jeffrey, and Lacey

Bernadette Peters: Kramer (Chow and Golden Retriever mix)

Candice Bergen: Lois (Basset/terrier mix) and Larry (spaniel mix)

Charlize Theron: Denver and Delilah

Courtney Love: Ronnie

David Duchovny: Blue (Collie/terrier mix)

Drew Barrymore: Flossie (Labrador/Chow mix)

Hilary Swank: Karoo (Jack Russell/Corgi mix)

Jackie Joyner-Kersee: Travis and Annie

Janet Jackson: Puffy

Jennifer Aniston: Norman (Corgi/terrier mix)

Lilly Allen: Honey

Matthew McConaughey: Miss Hudd (Labrador/Chow mix)

Orlando Bloom: Sidi

President Abraham Lincoln: Fido

President John F. Kennedy: Wolf

President Lyndon B. Johnson: Yuki

Sandra Bullock: Kernie and Bob

Senator John McCain: Coco

Sienna Miller: Porgy and Bess

Whether heroes and celebrities in their own right or the devoted companions of people from all walks of life, from presidents to the family next door, mixes are one-of-a-kind dogs who have made their way into the hearts and homes of those whose lives they enrich every day.

Although some of the following popular designer dog crosses have been around for many years, breeders still usually have to create these dogs by breeding two purebreds of the original breeds:

- Cockapoo: A cross of an American Cocker Spaniel and a Miniature or Toy Poodle. This cross has been around for a few decades and has its own national club with a code of ethics for its breeders. Cockapoos are small and have wavy hair and an affectionate personality.
- Labradoodle: An Australian creation using the Labrador Retriever and the Standard Poodle. The idea was to create a dog who could be trained as a service dog but didn't shed or cause allergy problems. These dogs are intelligent but active and a bit difficult to train. Appearance varies, but they are slightly large, with wavy or wiry coats and a square build.
- Puggle: A Beagle crossed with a Pug. Some people find this indescribable combination very cute. Other owners find this high-energy, feisty dog too much to handle. Puggles are small and have an unusually shaped head. They are

often tan with black markings.
- Yorkshire, Bichon, Toy Poodle, Maltese, or Miniature Schnauzer Crosses: This group of toys is used frequently to breed some of the most popular toy designer dogs. Looks vary widely, but dogs have a long or wavy coat. Personality may include the best—or worst—traits of the parent breeds. Health depends on the purebred parents and their backgrounds.

Best Furever Friend

Getting a dog is a lifetime commitment, so it's important to choose a mix that works with your lifestyle and abilities. A mix is likely to behave like the breeds in his background, so learn about those temperaments to see whether they're a good fit.

Don't just pick the cutest mutt at the shelter or the one who appears to be the most hopeless. Spend time with potential adoptees. Are your energy levels similar? Can you work with a boisterous or shy dog? Is it love at first sight—for both of you? Be sure that you are prepared and willing to provide the time, resources, and love necessary to fulfill the dog's needs, both physical and emotional, for the rest of his life.

Chapter 2

The Stuff of

Everyday Life

Adopting a new dog is an excellent excuse for a shopping spree. You'll need supplies and furnishings for him, and he will love being showered with toys and goodies. There is an almost limitless selection of dog gear from which to choose. So make up your list, set your budget, and go have fun getting ready for your new dog!

Bed

Your dog wants to be comfortable at night (and for naps) just as you do. Even if he ends up sleeping on your bed with you, he still needs his own bed.

Dog beds range from thin but cushy pads to thickly-padded contoured furniture and everything in between. A puppy or young dog might chew on his bed, so strong, resistant fabric and stuffing is your best choice. Older or arthritic dogs might prefer an orthopedic bed.

Heavy-coated dogs might not like warm, fluffy covers, while small or short-haired dogs would enjoy the added warmth. At any age, dogs drool, bring in outdoor dirt, or have accidents on their beds, so one that is washable and dryable allows the easiest maintenance.

Your dog's bed should be placed in a quiet, restful place, such as your bedroom or an unused guest room. It shouldn't be near outside doors or in drafty areas during cooler months. Wherever it's placed, your dog's bed should remain his alone, a spot for him to safely relax.

Bowls

From simple stainless steel to artsy ceramics, food and water bowls are available to match any home's decor. Before choosing design, though, pick the size that suits your dog's muzzle, height, and appetite.

Stainless bowls are long wearing, easy to sanitize, and available in the widest range of sizes. Unless they have a no-skid rubber bottom, they're dishwasher-safe. But don't put them in the microwave. Food that needs warming will have to be heated in a different bowl.

Your dog's bed should be placed in a quiet, restful place where he can feel calm and secure.

Ceramic bowls are the most visually appealing, but be certain that they are certified safe for use with food. If not, lead used in glazes may leach into food. Most ceramics are dishwasher- and microwave-safe, but check before purchase.

Plastic bowls are less expensive, but won't last as long. Some owners report that their dogs develop a rash on their faces or that their coats change color after prolonged use of plastics for drinking or eating containers. Cleanliness can also be a problem with plastic as it ages because it may chip, peel, or break down, allowing bacteria to build up. However, plastic bowls may be useful for traveling as they are not easily broken or dented.

Purchase at least two or three sets of bowls for your dog. That way one is always clean while another set is in use, and you have a spare set for outdoor play time or travel.

Crate

Crates may be made out of wire, plastic, nylon fabric, even wood furniture or decorative wicker. Four to six sizes are usually offered in each type.

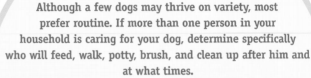

Setting Up a Schedule for Your Dog

Although a few dogs may thrive on variety, most prefer routine. If more than one person in your household is caring for your dog, determine specifically who will feed, walk, potty, brush, and clean up after him and at what times.

Adult dogs usually do best with two meals a day, while puppies need to be fed more often. Your dog will also need to go out each time he eats, at least once or twice during the remainder of the day, and maybe during the night.

In the real world, schedules have a way of falling apart when plans go awry or an unexpected problem occurs. Help your dog adapt to changes by teaching him to be a bit flexible in his schedule. Your dog depends on you for all his care. Regardless of how busy you are, always make certain your dog has what he needs first.

First choose the material that's safest for your dog, then one that functions well for your home and activities. If you travel with this crate, weight and compactability should be considered. A crate needs to be large enough for your dog to stand, turn, and lie in comfortably, but small enough that there is no room for him to eliminate in a corner.

Before buying a crate, inspect it for safety. Material should be resistant to chewing. The interior should be free of zippers, handles, or loops that could be chewed and swallowed, or in which your puppy could become entangled. Spacing between wires or other openings should be sized so your dog can't escape through or get caught in them. Your dog's crate should also be escape proof.

Line the crate with a soft, washable bottom. Carpet samples with a fleece liner or another bed are good choices.

Collar and Leash

Collars are like jewelry—as varied, personal, and flashy as you like. But collars also need to be practical and safe.

Size is the first consideration. Measure your dog's neck and add about 2 inches (5 cm). As your puppy grows up, you'll need to buy increasingly larger collars. A general suggestion is to choose a collar that when fastened allows you to easily slip two or three fingers underneath it.

Fasteners are the next decision. Buckle, break-away, and slip/training are the most common options. Slip collars are never meant to be left on a dog and should only be used by professional trainers. Break-away collars can prevent your dog from strangulation if he gets caught

on something. Buckles don't unfasten themselves if your dog becomes tangled, but if he's an escape artist, a buckle may be best.

Consider using a harness if your mix is small, prone to throat problems, or if he has orthopedic issues or arthritis.

Leashes are mostly made from nylon or leather, or a combination of these materials. The material you select depends on the strength of your dog, where you'll be walking him, and your preference for how it feels in your hand. Chain leashes are seldom a good choice because they can break or cause injury.

The length of the leash depends on your dog's height relative to who is walking him. Most daily-use leashes are around 5 or 6 feet

A collar needs to be properly fitted for safety and comfort.

(1.5 or 1.8 m), but are offered in slightly shorter or longer sizes. Long retractable leashes are handy for training or recreational activities.

Exercise Pen

Also called "X-pens," these collapsible fencing units are the equivalent of human playpens. X-pens can be used indoors to provide more room than a crate (if your puppy is housetrained already), or outdoors where no permanent fence is available. X-pens are handy if you like to camp with your dog. Choose a height that your dog cannot climb or jump over. Ventilated covers, to provide shade, may also be purchased for most pens.

Gate

Until your dog is well behaved, chances are you will want to keep him in one room or out of another. Preventing access to danger zones, like steep steps, is another reason to get a tension-mounted gate for your dog. And if you have cats, a gate can keep your dog out of their territory.

Gates can be purchased as baby gates or specifically as pet gates. Pet gates offer some model types that aren't available as baby gates, but are usually more expensive. Measure the opening you need to block in order to select the correct width. Height is determined by your dog's height and his ability to climb or jump.

Grooming Supplies

Because fur comes in a wide variety of lengths and types, dog owners may

FAMILY-FRIENDLY TIP

Your Children's Pet Care Responsibilities

Do you ask your children to care for themselves? No. You are the parent, and the same holds true for your dog. Although your children should share in your dog's care, they should never be primarily responsible. They can help by measuring out kibble at mealtime, scooping the poop, or brushing when you groom your dog. Depending on a child to supervise and carry out your pet's care places too much burden on young shoulders, even with older children. Kids get busy, forget, or don't understand how important these chores are, and your dog suffers. But asking them to assist with dog care teaches them compassion toward animals and responsible enjoyment of your family's canine companion.

have access to more beautifying tools than do people. The tools that are best for your mix depend on how much fur he has and what you need to do to it to maintain clean hair and skin.

Most dogs shed, so you'll need some type of device to remove loose fur. Longhaired dogs need detangling, double-coated dogs need dead undercoat removed. Do you

SENIOR DOG TIP

Adopting an Older Dog

Change may be upsetting for older dogs, but with love and a little time, most adapt well to new situations. If you're adopting an older dog, he'll need time to get over his past. First, make introductions between existing pets slowly. Don't just let the pets loose: Supervise the interaction and keep it short. Gradually lengthen the time they're together. Keep them separated while you're away until you're certain they get along and can be together safely. Show your new dog around his home and yard. Go out with him for potty breaks and praise him for eliminating in the correct spot. Set up an area that is his alone for eating and sleeping. Provide him with his own bed, bowls, and toys. Let him know that existing pets were there first and are going to stay. But spend plenty of time petting him, talking softly to him, and letting him know that he is welcome, loved, and has a permanent good home.

need to dry your dog's coat? Is he short and more easily groomed on a table? Along with coat care, all dogs need their nails trimmed and teeth brushed regularly.

Consider taking your mix to a professional groomer, and ask what type of shampoo or conditioner you need as well as which tools you should purchase. Ask what you need in combs, brushes, rakes, blades, trimmers, clippers, grinders, driers, and finishing tools such as slickers. Pet supply stores offer several options of medium-priced implements, while high-quality grooming tools can be ordered from specialty catalogs.

Identification

One of the most important purchases ever made for your dog is some form of identification. Regardless of training, every dog has the potential to escape or accidentally get loose. If your mix gets away, identification is his ticket home.

Although some counties can find an owner via a dog license, don't count on this alone. Place a set of ID tags with your telephone number and location on your dog's collar. Also consider having him microchipped or tattooed. These permanent forms of ID can be used to get your dog back to you if he loses his collar.

Microchips are injected under your dog's skin between the shoulders and are detected by scanners used in animal shelters and veterinary clinics. Tattooing can be done on your dog's inner flank or belly, preferably while he's being altered. Numbers are registered

Home-Alone Pets

If your dog is home alone all day, you'll need to make arrangements for his care, including midday potty breaks. Two options are hiring a pet sitter or dog walker, or taking your dog to an animal day care center.

Sitters and walkers come into your home to care for your dog. Walkers may only exercise your dog, and do this at the same time they walk other people's dogs. Pet sitters can be hired to do just about everything you're not there to do: water, feed, medicate, exercise, and even play with your dog on a one-to-one basis. Because a sitter spends time in your home, look for a trustworthy individual with strong pet knowledge and concern for your dog, and be sure to check references.

Doggy day care could be fun for your dog if he's outgoing and loves to be with other dogs. Before entrusting your pet to a day care center, make a visit to the facility. Observe other dogs to see whether they are happy, healthy, and under control. Interview staff to make certain they are qualified to work with multiple dogs and provide your pet with plenty of individual attention.

Sitters and centers should be insured, bonded, and prepared for emergencies. Key to choosing well is that your dog is happy with these options while you're away.

with identification bureaus, where your current contact information is maintained. Your registration fee includes contacting you when your dog is found.

Toys

Buying toys for your dog's enjoyment is one of the delights of pet ownership. There are more dog toys on the market than can be described, but they usually fall into five types: stuffies (soft stuffed toys), chew toys, catch or chase toys, treat toys, and toys that help train.

When buying a toy for your dog, always keep safety in mind first. Make sure the toy is bigger than his mouth so it can't be swallowed. Avoid small pieces that can break off and choke him, or ones that might cause an obstruction. Chew toys made from animal materials should be free of contaminants.

Dogs may be picky about what types of toys they enjoy, so try a variety. Some dogs will destroy softer toys and may do better with toys made from tough materials like rubber or ripstop nylon. When a toy wears out, replace it with a new one to prevent harm and replenish fun.

Licenses

Your dog doesn't need a license to drive, but he'll probably be required by your state or local government to have a dog license. Some counties verify that dogs are licensed and may confiscate those who are not. Licenses can also be used as secondary identification if your dog becomes lost. In most counties, it is a legal requirement to keep a license tag on your dog's collar along with his identification tag.

Exercise for Good Health

Exercise—or the lack of it—is always in the news, with health care authorities urging people to exercise more to stay fit. The same is true for your dog, in some ways more so because recreational exercise is such a huge and necessary portion of his daily life.

Exercise keeps joints and muscles moving, keeps calories from packing on as fat, and establishes a metabolism that builds good health for a long life. It also prevents your dog from becoming mentally dull, not to mention that he'll be happier with plenty of physical play in his life.

Your mix may be from breeds that are highly energetic. If so, you'll need to plan daily activities, like ball or fetch, that burn off his extra energy. Mixes that come from couch-potato-type breeds still need exercise. Casual walks several times weekly or indoor hide-and-seek games should meet your sedate dog's needs just fine.

The bonus to exercising your dog is that your health can improve too. More importantly, the time you spend playing together builds and strengthens the bond between you and your pet.

Chapter **3**

Eating Well

The health of your dog depends on what he eats—
which constitute the foods you choose to feed him
and those you do not allow him to eat. Poor-quality
food can cause or worsen many health conditions,
including allergies, digestive disorders, and thyroid
disease. But a diet of premium ingredients can
make your dog's coat shine, his eyes sparkle,
and put a bounce in his step for many years.
In addition to training, there is nothing more
important you can do for you dog than to feed him
a complete and balanced diet.

Basic Canine Nutrition

The best way to ensure that your dog eats properly is to offer him food that provides all the nutrients he needs to maintain a healthy and a sound body. The basic components of a nutritious canine diet consist primarily of carbohydrates, fats, proteins, vitamins, minerals, and water, which, in the proper combination, fuel growth, energy, and body repair. Proteins are essential building blocks for your dog's growth and development. Carbohydrates provide energy. Fats provide energy, transport vitamins, and insulate and protect organs. Minerals and vitamins regulate body processes. Water, most essential to life, is needed for every bodily function;

it aids in digestion and the transport of nutrients, helps remove toxins and waste from the body, and regulates body temperature. Whether feeding a commercial food or a homemade diet, offering optimal nutrition is the most important factor toward maintaining your dog's good health and longevity.

Reading Food Labels

Commercial pet foods are overseen by The Association of American Feed Control Officials (AAFCO). This organization analyzes dog foods to see whether they meet the minimum requirements of total nutrient amounts and ratios. Before it can claim that a product is complete and balanced, a manufacturer must have received

A well-balanced, nutritious diet will help your dog look and feel his best.

approval for that claim from the AAFCO. The phrase "complete and balanced" means that all necessary nutrients—substances essential to life that must be obtained from food—are present in the correct amounts and proportions. Although you should feed a food that is AAFCO approved, this certification does not mean that a food is necessarily the best choice for your dog.

You'll have to read labels carefully to find the food that is right for your mix. Ingredient listings can be difficult to understand, so learn as much as you can about the contents of dog food. The AAFCO controls which ingredients can be used and how, and the Food and Drug Administration's Center for Veterinary Medicine sets the guidelines for defining an ingredient. Label information should include a Guaranteed Analysis chart, which shows how much content, in percentages, a dog food has in protein, carbohydrates, fats, fiber, and water. Ingredients must be labeled accurately and are listed in descending order of quantity, with greatest amounts first. Remember that three listings for grain may end up equaling more than a meat ingredient listed first. (e.g., beef, rice bran, rice hulls, and whole rice).

Foods that use high-quality ingredients manufactured to preserve the nutrients take the guesswork out of feeding your dog a nutritious, balanced diet. Less expensive foods can use ingredients from sources that have been rejected as unfit for human consumption. They often include harmful preservatives, artificial flavors or colors, chemical binders, or nonnutritive fillers that your dog doesn't need and may be harmful to his health.

To learn what ingredient definitions mean, go to the AAFCO or FDA-CVM websites. For questions about a specific product, contact the manufacturer.

Commercial Foods

Do you have time to cook for your dog? Do you know exactly which nutrients he needs and in what proportions and which foods to use to get these nutrients? Like most owners, the answer to these questions is probably "No." Buying your dog's food off the shelf is the simplest way you can ensure that his diet is balanced and that you'll always have a meal ready for him.

Multiple Dogs

Mealtime etiquette for multiple dogs can be thought of as a formal dinner party, where every guest has an assigned seat. Despite their nature to get along well with other pets, each dog needs his own, separate bowl and eating space. Individual crates or feeding areas in the kitchen and other rooms work well for this. Separation during dinner will keep each dog from having to share his meal, and thus prevent any growling, snapping or hoarding from ever getting started. It's also the only way to make certain that any dogs on a special diet get exactly the food they are supposed to eat.

Eating Well

Dry Foods

Dry food, or kibble, is the most popular dog food offered to consumers and the staple in most dogs' diets. It's easy to feed and convenient to store and, once opened, remains fresh for long periods of time, if stored in a sealable bin or airtight bag.

Kibble comes in an endless variety of flavors, ingredients, and types. Your dog shouldn't have to settle for a food that is nutritious but unpleasant tasting or one that tastes great but isn't healthy. A premium-quality food that is both healthy and tasty costs more. But consider it an investment in your dog's health: The better the food, the better his health, which means fewer veterinary expenses.

Kibble is composed of meat (muscles, organs, fats, or by-products like ligaments) for protein and fat, grain to hold the mixture together (whole grain is best), vegetables, fruits (carbohydrates), and vitamins and minerals. The grade, source, and wholeness (versus a portion of) these ingredients is what determines the quality of the food.

Less expensive products are made from discarded meats or by-product grains graded unfit for human consumption. Soybean or corn meal, animal digest, and meat by-products from an unnamed meat source are used as the main ingredients. Other ingredients that have no nutritional value are often added, including sugars, salts, artificial colors, flavoring, chemical binders, and preservatives that may be harmful.

The manufacturing process also affects quality. Kibble baked

Make sure fresh water is available for your dog.

quickly at high temperatures (which is more cost-efficient to make) causes naturally-occurring vitamins and minerals to break down and become unavailable. Supplements must then be sprayed on in a coating of fat, which in cheaper foods can come from leftover restaurant grease. Healthier dry foods use high-grade ingredients and are manufactured to preserve nutrients.

With a rising demand for healthier food for pets, the quality of ingredients in dog food today has greatly improved. Premium-quality kibble uses whole grains, vegetables, and healthier meat parts that would be safe enough for you to eat. These products are more digestible and the nutrients more absorbable. The result is better health for your dog.

Feeding Kibble

Dry food typically makes up from 70 to 90 percent of a dog's diet. Treats, canned food, and other healthy foods added in make up the rest. Most vets recommend that once you find a dry food your dog likes and is healthy for him, stick with it. Changes should be made gradually to avoid digestive upsets, unless your vet instructs otherwise.

Feeding amounts vary greatly by the size of your dog, his activity level, and how energy-dense (protein and calorie content) the food is. Small mixes may eat as little as one-half cup (227 g) a day while giant dogs might need as much as four cups (1.4 kg) daily.

Canned Foods

Canned food is mostly liquid—about 70 to 85 percent water or broth—so is also called "soft" or "moist" food. Besides moisture, canned dog food normally

Supplements

A supplement is a concentrated, combined, or isolated version of nutrients provided as nutritional aids. They can consist of vitamins, minerals, amino acids, and digestive enzymes, prepared separately or in various combinations. Premium-quality dog foods normally contain the correct amount and ratio of these ingredients, making supplementation unnecessary. Excess or unbalanced amounts of added vitamins and minerals can be toxic.

If you have to add supplements to your dog's meals for him to be healthy, that's a sign your food is not meeting his needs. Find a better food that contains the necessary ingredients.

Your vet may advise you to give your dog supplements temporarily if he is recovering from an illness or injury. For example, some orthopedic conditions like arthritis may be helped with glucosamine and chondroitin, and skin issues may be improved with fatty acids. Before adding a supplement, however, have your vet tell you which one to use, how much, and how often.

contains meat, meat fat, a small portion of grains, vegetables, and maybe fruit, vitamins, and minerals. Some specially canned food may be grain-free or reduced-fat.

Because canning is a food preservation method, artificial preservatives are seldom added to canned food. Shelf life for cans is several months. However, once a can is opened, it must be covered, refrigerated, and kept for no longer than three or four days.

Like kibble, premium canned food contains ingredients from quality sources and has few nonnutritive additives. Less expensive brands use poorer-quality meat scraps and may include soy fillers instead of wholesome grains.

Canned food may also contain artificial enhancers, brighteners, unnecessary sugars, salts, or artificial thickeners. Some seasonings, like onion powder, also may be unhealthy for your dog.

Most dogs love the taste and smell of canned dog foods. A finicky eater can often be persuaded to eat by having some soft food stirred into his kibble. Dogs who need extra liquid or fat in their diet can also have canned food added to their kibble.

Feeding Canned Foods

You can include about 20 to 25 percent canned food as part of your dog's daily feedings. A few dogs with certain dental, digestive, or urinary tract problems may eat canned food exclusively if your vet recommends this. But canned food makes for dirtier teeth than does kibble, so brush your dog's teeth more often.

Moist food goes a long ways—a few spoonfuls per meal are enough. Too much can cause diarrhea, gas, and rapid weight gain. Buy soft food in large cans for multiple dogs or large dogs, small cans for toy mixes. But beware: Content

A carefully designed home-cooked diet can have many advantages for a dog with special needs.

is more important than fancy names or labeling.

Semi-Moist Foods

Semi-moist products look like beef chunks or ground hamburger. They stay fresh for a long time, but they have a down side. Semi-moist foods are more expensive and are loaded with ingredients that have no nutritional value, and some that can be harmful.

The natural-looking meat color is achieved by using artificial colors. And the flavor comes from a high level of hidden salts, sugars, and artificial flavors. Unbalanced and excess sodium and sugar are implicated in multiple health problems including kidney and heart disease, tooth decay, diabetes, and obesity.

In order to retain their 20 to 25 percent moisture content, preservatives like propylene glycol are included. Propylene glycol (a chemical cousin to the poisonous ethylene glycol) is a gooey liquid used in the manufacturing of plastics and paint solvents.

If semi-moist foods aren't a healthy choice, why are they made? Because they appeal to owners who want to feel they're giving their dogs a special food. If you want to feed your dog something special, spend your money on the best kibble you can buy.

Treats

The snack of the doggy world, treats are probably available in as many flavors as there are types of dogs. Because treats are not meant as a component of a regular diet, they are

Changing Your Dog's Diet

Although some dogs need to stay on one food for their lifetime, other dogs prefer and do fine with a little variety. But don't just switch your dog's food suddenly; a rapid change may cause digestive upsets. Slowly mix in a little of the new food while reducing the amount of the original feed each day.

33

not made with nutrition in mind. They are meant to appeal to doggy taste buds—and to owners' hearts when they make their dog happy by feeding him a treat.

Treats are made using the same variety of ingredients and additives that are used in dry kibble and semi-moist foods. But they tend to have more flavorings and color added, and are usually higher in fat, sugars, sodium—and calories! Because of this, a slight reduction in quantity of main food should be made in your dog's diet to allow for the additional caloric intake if you are going to give him treats.

If your mix is allergic, or on a special diet for health conditions like urinary stones or pancreatitis, treats must be selected with extra care.

Avoid adding any ingredients to which your dog might react or which could exacerbate his problem. It is best to consult with your veterinarian in these circumstances about what types of treats you can offer and how often.

It is possible to buy healthy, lower calorie, more "natural" treats. Dry treats are preferable over moist ones because they are better for teeth and may contain less artificial additives. Just read labels closely when selecting a healthy treat for your dog. Or offer him a baby carrot, or a couple blueberries.

Noncommercial Foods

Home-cooked and raw diets are being prepared by more owners concerned about the quality and source of the ingredients in commercial pet foods. If you share these concerns and have the time and motivation to prepare your dog's food yourself, some research and effort can provide your dog with a personalized diet.

Home-Cooked Foods

Before you cook for your dog, learn what he needs nutritionally. Buy a book with suggested recipes and nutritional statistics on various foods. Shop for high-quality produce, then put it together in your own kitchen. If your dog has special health considerations, cooking his food can tailor his diet to his specific

needs and help you avoid ingredients that cause problems.

Home-prepared dog foods can be as basic as cooking an extra portion of the same healthy meats, vegetables, fruits, and grain products that you serve your family. Feeding leftover table scraps that you wouldn't eat does not count as home-cooked dog food. Your dog's meals need to be just as healthy as yours are—or should be.

You can use a variety of lean-cut meats, eggs, or a limited quantity of dairy products to make up between 10 and 30 percent of the food. Complex carbohydrates (vegetables, fruits, and whole grains) should make up about 25 to 45 percent of the food, and the balance should be a healthy source of fat.

Pay attention to calcium levels in homemade food—it is difficult to get the correct amount without bone. But don't use whole bones because they are dangerous. Measure in bone meal or a low-fat, lactose-reduced dairy product such as yogurt. Fats can come from meat or oils such as olive or canola.

Refrigerate or freeze unused portions, and discard unused portions remaining after three days in the fridge or two months in the freezer. Don't use foods that have been shown to be hazardous for dogs. This list can include onions, chocolate, grapes, raisins, corn oil, and some nuts. Some dogs may also have problems with additional foods, so to start, try only a few ingredients in each recipe until you know which ones your dog tolerates well.

When cooking for your dog, you need to monitor his weight closely until you determine the correct amount to feed him. If he's gaining weight but still hungry after eating, ingredients need to be adjusted. Also observe his coat, skin, bowel habits, and energy level. If he doesn't look or act normal, it's time for a change in diet. Good health, on the other hand, says you're on the right track.

How often you feed your dog is determined by his age, health, and activity level.

Raw Food Diets

Another option in home-prepared dog food is raw meat and uncooked vegetables. The raw diet, known as BARF (biologically appropriate raw foods), is supposed to be similar to what a dog (or wolf) would eat in the wild. Proponents of BARF believe that the canine digestive system was designed to eat a raw diet that, when reproduced at home, results in a healthier dog.

Meat (chicken, turkey, lamb, or beef, but never pork or fish) makes up about two-thirds of the meal, and fresh vegetables the rest. Grains, like oats or whole rice, and fruits are sometimes added, usually after blending in a food processor. It is necessary to include raw bones for the calcium your dog needs.

Owners who feed this diet swear by its results. But there are numerous risks. Raw meat is a haven for harmful bacteria and possibly parasites. A dog's digestive system is better equipped to kill off the bacteria, but your dog can still become quite ill from eating (or you from handling) raw meat.

Meat must be cut fresh at the store each time it's needed, then chopped or ground further at home. Meals then

FAMILY-FRIENDLY TIP

Kids Feeding Dogs

Don't count on a child to remember to feed the dog—that's your job. Dogs can get overly excited or territorial about their food, so it's important to teach your dog and child how to work together safely at doggy mealtime.

Always have your dog sit and wait for his bowl to be put down. Your child can help by measuring out the food while your dog is waiting. Be certain your child understands that she should never bother your dog while he's eating or try to take his food away. Your dog should also be trained to allow his food to be removed without fussing.

Don't allow children to give treats unless you determine the amount and type. Show them how to give the treat from an open, flat palm so your dog can't accidentally mouth their fingers. Young children often drop or hand over their own food to the family dog, so just as you would do during family mealtimes, put your dog in his crate while you feed your toddler.

must be packaged individually and frozen. Prepared foods may be kept frozen for only a short time. And all tools and counter surfaces must be carefully washed and sterilized after preparation.

Raw bones are given separately if not ground into the meat-veggie mixture. Even though raw bones are softer, there is still a very real danger that they can splinter and cause serious damage to your dog's mouth or digestive tract.

The risks of a raw diet are great, including the possibility of severe illness, injury, or even death. But the payoff may also be great if your dog doesn't do well on other diets. Before feeding raw, discuss the option in detail with your veterinarian.

If you decide to feed raw foods, thoroughly educate yourself first on how and what to feed. You can choose to offer only a raw diet, or as with home-cooked dog meals, you can supplement kibble with BARF a few times weekly. You might also consider buying a foundation product from a pet supply store to use as the base for the raw mixture. If you feed raw, be thorough and careful with your preparation, and switch your dog's food gradually.

Feeding Schedules

Most dogs are creatures of habit. They like to know that at a certain time each day their food dish is filled and set in front of them. But real life is frequently interrupted by unplanned circumstances. Your dog needs regular meals daily, but it helps if he can adapt to some change in routine.

How often you feed your dog is

determined by his age, health, and activity level. Puppies need to be fed three to four times daily, with the number of meals reduced as they grow. Adults usually do best with two feedings a day, one in the morning and another in the evening. Senior dogs may need smaller meals more often, just like pups, or may continue to do well with two daily meals.

Whatever age, try to space feedings evenly over a 12-hour period. For dogs who eat more than twice daily, meals can be spread over 14 to 16 hours. Toy-sized dogs may not be able to get enough calories from two meals and can develop hypoglycemia (low blood sugar). If your dog is tiny, he may need three meals, or midday and bed-time snacks. An older dog may also need a snack before bedtime.

Free-Feeding

Some dogs don't adhere well to schedules. These dogs prefer meals on their terms. A dog who is thin, or finicky, can eat only a little at a time, perhaps due to a health problem (like a sore mouth), or one who is very active and needs energy often might thrive on free-feeding.

Free-feeding means that dry food is available at all times. It doesn't mean leaving food out until it spoils, or putting new food in the bowl with old leftovers. Having food available at all times provides your dog with the opportunity to eat when he's hungry, then stop when he's had enough.

There are, however, exceptions. An overweight dog should never be allowed access to food at all times because he won't stop eating on his own. Scheduled, controlled meals are best for him. If you have more than one dog, free-feeding can result in fights for the food dish. Dogs with calm dispositions who are used to nibbling can still do fine. But be sure to provide

SENIOR DOG TIP

Feeding the Senior Dog

As a dog ages, his nutritional needs and ability to digest food decline. Some dogs require fewer calories when they become less active, while others need more calories because they eat less as they grow older. Age-related disease can also change nutritional needs. Special foods with prescribed limits of proteins, sodium, fats, or other nutrients may be necessary if your older dog has kidney, heart, or other organ failure disease.

Weight loss or loss of appetite is seldom a sign of normal aging. Have your senior dog examined by your vet if this happens. She can run tests and determine whether your dog needs a prescription diet as part of the treatment plan.

Table Manners

At first, a dog begging for food may seem cute, but that cute look eventually progresses to pawing and barking, and maybe stealing your food. Begging can become annoying to you (and your guests), and it is not a healthy or acceptable behavior.

Stop begging before it begins. When it's the family's dinnertime, put your dog in his crate, either with a safe toy or his own meal. Or block him from the kitchen while you eat. Use the *down* and stay commands to keep him out of your food if he is near your table or tray while you snack or eat more casually. Never feed him from your plate.

If your dog whimpers or barks, ignore him. For more persistent behavior, tell him "enough" and continue ignoring him while you eat. He'll learn his antics don't gain the desired response.

If your dog's strong desire for human food further prompts him to begin food stealing when you are not present, help him resist temptation by never leaving anything within reach—on kitchen tables, countertops, etc.—which is unreasonably tempting for any canine.

Make proper food management part of your training routine by establishing appropriate feeding habits right from the start—your dog will be healthier and happier if you reinforce good manners.

a separate full dish for each dog.

Serve only the amount of food your dog will eat during 24 hours. Each morning, discard what remains and wash or replace the bowl with a clean one and fresh food. A free-fed dog should still have regular outdoor time to empty his bowels each morning and night.

Obesity

A chubby dog is not cute, healthy, or happy. According to the American Veterinary Medical Association, the fourth leading cause of death in dogs is disease related to obesity! A dog that's only 10 percent overweight may have his life span reduced by one-third. The higher his weight, the shorter his life and the greater his health problems. About 65 percent of the dogs a vet sees are being treated for problems related to obesity.

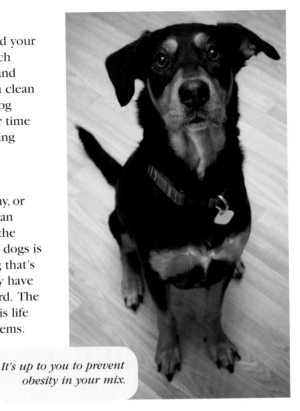

It's up to you to prevent obesity in your mix.

If these numbers don't scare you into keeping your dog slender, consider the discomfort he'll experience (and the money you'll spend on vet care) if he develops early arthritis, torn ligaments, shortness of breath, heart disease, high blood pressure, diabetes, pancreatitis, bladder stones, or cancer—conditions caused or aggravated by excess weight. And obese dogs are at greater risk for stroke, heat exhaustion, and surgical complications.

Monitor you dog's weigh regularly. If you can't feel his ribs or see his waste, cut back on his daily rations. Some mixes are more prone to weight gain than others and need fixed portions of lower-calorie foods to prevent weight gain. Older dogs may gain weight more easily as they become less active.

One of the best ways you can love your dog is to keep him at a healthy weight. Food is not love; feeding your dog human snack (junk) food, extra treats, or too much dog food will kill him. Love him enough not to overfeed him and to provide him with regular exercise.

Chapter 4

Looking Good

Dog grooming is comparable to your own daily beauty and hygiene regimen. Being clean contributes to your dog's overall health and also makes him look and feel good. Plus it's a time when you're touching and handling your dog, which is one of the best ways to be close and show him how much you love and care about him.

Being clean contributes to your dog's overall health and also makes him look and feel good

Coat and Skin Care

There's no single specific way for you to groom a mixed-breed dog because each mix's fur is unique. But there are a few basic coat types that your mix may have: shorthaired or smooth-coated (Labrador, Beagle); longhaired, which can be straight or wavy (Cocker Spaniel, Newfoundland); double-coated, which is a stiff outer coat with a shorter soft undercoat (German Shepherd, Siberian Husky); wirehaired (most terriers); and curly-coated (Poodle, Bichon). Whatever combination your dog's coat is, he needs regular bathing and brushing—and maybe more.

Shorthaired/Smooth-Coated Dogs

Shorthaired and smooth-coated dogs shed continuously. The best way to manage shedding is through bathing and frequent brushing. Although this is the easiest coat to groom, don't neglect it. A quick twice-weekly brushing keeps short coats glossy and healthy.

Bathing and Drying

These are wet, lather, rinse, and good-to-go dogs. Their coats air dry in a short time. You can towel off excess water or blow dry on a cool temperature setting if the weather is chilly. How often you bathe your dog depends on how naturally oily his skin and coat are, and if he's gotten dirty while playing, but you may give him a bath as often as once a week.

Brushing

Use a slicker, stiff-bristled brush, grooming glove, or a rubber comb to keep the short coat looking glossy. These tools are also good for removing dead, shedding hair before it gets onto your clothing.

Longhaired Dogs

Long coats may be thin (Yorkie) or thick (Collie), but both mat easily and require a dedicated effort to keep them tangle-free. Just as human hair needs to be cut, longhaired dogs need to be clipped or the coat continues to grow. You can groom your longhaired dog yourself, but getting a groomer to show you how may make the job easier.

Bathing and Drying

Care must be taken not to tangle the coat while bathing a longhaired dog. Prior to bathing, comb out any large mats because wetting can tighten them. Wet the coat thoroughly. To prevent tangling, mix and dilute your shampoo so you can pour it over the entire coat rather than scrubbing it into a lather. Use a softening shampoo and a detangling conditioner. Shampoo and rinse only in the direction of the hair. Rinse until the water runs clear. When finished, wring excess water out of the coat without twisting or bunching the hair. Use towels to absorb as much water as possible from the coat. Don't rub, just squeeze the hair as you would a sponge.

Next, blow dry the coat. Blow drying is a necessity with long coats—it's the only way to keep tangles from forming and get the skin completely dry. Hot spots or flaking develop if long fur is left damp next to the skin.

Use cool or barely warm temperature settings to dry. Start from the front, moving to the back, and next to the skin, moving out the ends of the hair. Separate and lift sections of hair, drying one section, from the skin out, before moving to the next. Use a steel-toothed comb to keep hair from tangling.

Grooming Supplies

Many different types of grooming tools and supplies are available at your local pet supply store or online, so have a groomer recommend which ones will work best for your mix's coat type. If you have the appropriate tools, grooming will be easier for both you and your dog. Here are the basics:

- shampoo, conditioner, extra bottles
- special ear or eye cleaners
- bath mat, cotton balls, towels, dryer
- clippers, scissors, nail trimmer
- brushes, combs, rakes (depending on coat type)
- doggy toothbrush, toothpaste
- powder, styptic powder
- box for storing supplies

Combing

Daily combing prevents mats and removes debris from the coat. If you can't comb daily, aim for three or four times a week. Most long coats are better maintained using a steel-toothed comb. Mat rakes help remove tangles that get ahead of you. Pay particular attention to areas where mats form, like armpits, backs of the legs, and around the collar, and where debris collects, like the feet, ears, beard, and fringe.

Double-Coated Dogs

Double-coated dogs "blow" coat at least twice a year and shed in between. This means the undercoat comes out in tufts and a new undercoat grows in. Some of the guard hair (the outer coat) is lost at this time too. Regardless, double-coated dogs are fairly easy maintenance, unless their outer coat is long (Keeshond, Pomeranian), in which case they would be groomed in the same manner as longhaired dogs.

Bathing and Drying

Baths control a coat blow because they hasten the process. In between baths, double coats repel and shed dirt and debris. But your dog should still be bathed at least monthly to keep his skin and coat healthy.

Use a hand-held sprayer to wet the coat from the underneath up, then the top down. Stop when water runs through rather than off the coat. Mix and dilute shampoo to pour on so that it's evenly distributed throughout the thick coat. Lather in the direction of coat growth. Although tangles are uncommon, scrubbing in a random

Choosing a Professional Groomer

Finding a qualified and caring professional to groom your dog should be undertaken with many of the same considerations you would apply in selecting a kennel or veterinarian. Important considerations include:

- Is the groomer certified by a reputable board?
- Does the groomer have sufficient experience in her trade?
- Is the grooming facility clean? Are the grooming implements cleaned between each use?
- Does the groomer competently and happily handle special requests?
- Do other dogs present appear relaxed, or are they anxious?
- Is the groomer considerate of and patient with the dogs on which she works?
- Is the groomer experienced with dogs, and does she understand canine behavior?
- Does the groomer like dogs and enjoy the work?
- Is the groomer willing to give you a tour, or meet your dog and talk with you before you make an appointment?

pattern can cause dead fur to tangle into the coat. A comb with large rubber nubs helps reach the skin, but brush in the direction of fur growth. Use a moisturizing conditioner and rinse thoroughly.

Towel dry by squeezing the fur, but do it without crumpling or twisting. Use a blow dryer on a cool setting to get the coat dry and loosen dead fur that wasn't removed by the bath. Work from back to front and bottom to top. This helps the coat stand out and gets air into the fur next to the skin. When the coat is almost dry, use an undercoat rake or shedding blade while finishing.

Brushing

Weekly brushing is usually enough to keep double coats looking good and dirt free. Brush more often if your dog is blowing coat. The best tools are undercoat rakes, pin brushes, and large-gapped steel combs. A slicker brush is a nice finish to glossy double coats.

Wirehaired Dogs

Wirehaired dogs, like terrier mixes, barely shed, only losing a little hair periodically. Wire coats are easily maintained from day to day, but a full grooming involves more skill. Dead hair must be removed because it doesn't shed out, and the coat needs to be shaped.

Bathing and Drying

Because their coats provide natural protection against dirt, dogs with wire coats don't need to be bathed frequently. Excessive bathing softens the coat and dries the skin. To shampoo, lather in the direction of fur growth so as not to tangle the coat. Use a moisturizing conditioner, but one that doesn't remove body from the fur.

Wring excess water from the fur without tangling it. Blow dry the coat to reduce matting. Comb it through with a rubber-tipped slicker while drying. Use low heat and low speed to prevent fluffing or tangling of the coat.

Trimming

Shaping the coat by trimming requires skill. Find a groomer or experienced owner to teach you how to do it properly, or buy a how-to DVD. You'll need electric clippers and a pair of blunt-tipped, good-quality scissors. Your dog may not have a perfect trim until you've had some practice, but just follow the lines of his body.

Don't trim a dirty coat. Trim after

a bath, but wait at least 30 to 60 minutes or until the coat is completely dry. Trimmer blades should be sharp or the hair will pull instead of cut. Allow about an hour or more for a total trim. Use the services of a groomer if you don't think you have the patience or time to do this yourself.

Grooming as a Health Check

Grooming sessions are the perfect time to give your dog a health check.

- Is his skin dry, flaky, or too oily? Are there any bald patches, hot spots, or other changes in skin color or appearance?
- Is his fur dry, brittle, or flaky?
- Are there fleas, ticks, or signs of other parasites?
- Are there new lumps or bumps?
- Does he wince or have pain when you touch him?
- Are his ears dirty? Do they have an unusual odor?
- Is his mouth inflamed? Is his breath foul smelling?
- Does he have cuts on his feet or debris between the pads?

If you find a problem, schedule a veterinary exam right away.

Combing and Stripping

A daily combing with a mat rake keeps debris out of a wiry coat and prevents mats from forming. Or you can use a steel-tooth comb or cat slicker for weekly coat maintenance.

Dead hair is removed by stripping it, either by plucking or clipping. You can use a flea comb to remove it or your fingers to pluck it. If you use a stripping blade, get a groomer to show you how to do this correctly.

Curly-Coated Dogs

Consider using a professional groomer if your mix has a curly coat. Curly fur grows quickly, tangles easily, and needs to be shaped by trimming. If you tackle the grooming yourself, get a how-to DVD or book, or search the Internet for detailed instructions and photos.

Bathing and Drying

Coats that curl are found in breeds that worked as water dogs. These coats are naturally oily, so choose a shampoo that doesn't dry the hair, thus allowing the coat to retain its natural oils. Use a conditioner that detangles and

47

Looking Good

SENIOR DOG TIP

Grooming Your Senior Dog

Although he may fuss more, regular grooming is as important for an older dog as it is for a young one. It's an opportunity to check the body for age-related changes in health and catch problems early. And your senior will feel, look, and smell better after being groomed. But keep your senior's comfort in mind. Older dogs tire more quickly and may have stiff, painful joints or tender skin. Use a lighter, gentler touch when grooming your senior. Keep sessions short, and let him take breaks or lie down when you work on one side. Don't do everything at once; spread the routine over two or three days.

it through the coat gently with your fingers until you have a light lather, then rinse. Curly coats may need two washings.

Wring water from curls by running your hands against the body from front to back, top to bottom. Soak up more water by squeezing with towels. If you want the coat to curl, dry it on a low speed without combing. To straighten curls, use a high-velocity dryer, blowing upward while combing with a wide-toothed mat rake or undercoat comb. Be aware that straightened curls mat more readily and must be protected from food, indoor lint, and outdoor dirt.

Combing and Clipping

To prevent mats and remove dead fur, comb at least weekly—but more often is better. A full clip should be done no less than once a month. A slicker, mat comb, or Poodle comb is the best tool for combing.

This coat type is the most difficult to trim correctly, so get help. Use a groomer, or practice with an experienced owner. Or consider keeping your curly dog in a close trim. A good set of trimmers and finishing scissors is essential.

Ear Care

Ears that are not regularly groomed can get painful infections that may lead to hearing loss. A good time to clean your dog's ears is after bathing him. Before putting him into the tub, though, place a cotton ball loosely in the entrance to the ear canal—this

moisturizes without softening. Frequent bathing—every two weeks—is needed to keep the oils from building up and to prevent your dog from developing a bad odor.

Wet the coat with a handheld sprayer. Dilute and pour the shampoo or apply it to a sponge, then your dog. Starting from the front and top, work reduces the chance of water running into his ear, which could also cause discomfort and infections.

While you're towel drying your dog, gently and carefully wipe the exterior of his ear flap and the outer area of the ear. Do not use pressure or wipe deeply inside the ear. If your dog's ears are very dirty, use a pet ear cleaner before his bath. Follow directions, then wipe with a towel.

Don't limit ear cleaning to bath time. If your mix has drop ears (floppy ears), they are more prone to build up dirt and become infected. Check them at least once a week. If you see a large amount of wax, remove it with a paper towel or tissue. For worse buildup, use an ear-cleaning product as directed.

Between cleanings, be aware of signs that your dog's ears may be bothering him. If he shakes his head, paws or scratches his ears frequently,

ducks his head or whimpers when you pet him, or his ears are red or have a foul odor, they might be infected. Never try to clean your dog's ears with swabs. Leave that to your veterinarian who can treat infections and clean the ears at the same time.

Some dogs have heavy hair growth inside their ears. This excess hair sometimes needs to be removed to reduce wax buildup or frequent infections. Get your vet or a groomer to show you how to pluck or trim this hair.

Eye Care

If your mix is white or light-colored, or if he has protruding-type eyes (Pugs), he may be prone to tearing and tear stains. But any dog can be affected by excess tears. Tearing can be caused by eye disease, allergies, or ingredients in your dog's food. Have your dog's eyes checked by his veterinarian if they

Inspect and clean your dog's ears and eyes as part of his regular grooming routine.

start tearing or show signs of redness or swelling. Some tears are caused by treatable medical conditions. If your vet determines that your dog is simply prone to tearing, you can keep his eyes clean during grooming sessions at home.

For regular cleaning, use a cotton ball moistened with warm water or saline solution to wash around the eye every few days. For tear stains on light coats, try a solution specifically made for pet tear-stain removal. Follow the manufacturer's directions. You may also apply a thin coating of petroleum jelly below the eyes once you've cleaned the stain. This keeps the tears from saturating the fur and reduces further discoloration. Mixes with longer fur around the eyes may benefit from having this hair carefully trimmed away.

Dental Care

Can you imagine how awful your mouth would taste and your teeth would look if you didn't brush daily? The same is true for your dog. Mixes that are tiny, or that have brachycephalic faces (Bulldogs), are more prone to dental problems, so clean teeth are crucial to their oral health.

Unbrushed teeth develop tartar and plaque, which lead to gingivitis, periodontal disease, and tooth decay or loss. Bacteria caused by these conditions can actually harm your

For good oral hygiene, brush your dog's teeth at least once a week.

dog's overall health and make him ill, possibly affecting his heart or kidneys. As an added bonus, keeping your dog's teeth clean will also prevent him from getting that nasty doggy breath and will make his kisses even more pleasant.

For good oral hygiene, you need to brush your mix's teeth after he eats to prevent food from sticking to and between them. Daily brushing is best, but if you can't manage that, two or three times a week is a recommended minimum. If you're really busy, give his chompers a thorough cleaning once each week at the very least.

How to Brush Your Dog's Teeth

Never use human toothpaste to brush your dog's teeth. Swallowing it can make your dog quite ill, and he certainly can't rinse and spit as you can. Ask your vet or pet supply store to recommend a doggy toothpaste; a flavored toothpaste such as chicken or peanut butter is often well received. Plus, some cleaners have enzymes to help break down plaque.

Buy a dog-specific brush sized for your pet's mouth. A children's brush may work in a pinch. If you don't want to use a standard bristled brush, try a rubber-nubbed brush that fits on your finger (these work well for smaller dogs).

Get your dog used to your working in his mouth. Start when he's young or, if he's an adult when you adopt him, as soon as he settles securely into your home. First wrap the end of a washcloth over your finger and just rub his teeth. Then move to a

Grooming Increases Bonding Time

Dogs love to be touched, and we like to hug and pet them, particularly when they're clean. You should find that the uninterrupted time spent grooming your dog is peaceful and relaxing for both of you. Even though grooming takes time, the investment in your dog's well-being pays off more than you can imagine as your bond builds while caring for him.

brush without toothpaste. When he accepts this, allow him to smell or lick the flavored toothpaste. Next place a small amount on a brush and start with his front teeth. Refill the brush, and move around to the sides. As brushing becomes routine, brush the inner side of his teeth as well. Don't use a treat for a reward (you've just cleaned food off his teeth!); praise your dog instead.

Oral Health Check

At least once a month, while you're brushing your dog's teeth, inspect his mouth for problems. Are his gums red? Is there a broken tooth? An unusual swelling or bad odor? If so, take your

Looking Good

dog to the vet for an oral exam. Also schedule a yearly appointment (or when your vet recommends) for a thorough professional cleaning, just as you do for your own teeth.

What a difference grooming made for this Peekapoo!

Nail Care

Nails that are too long are uncomfortable, and they cause your dog to slip when he walks. Long nails that are ripped out during high-speed running or in rough play can cause extreme pain. If they're trimmed, this won't happen.

Most dogs don't like the pinching sensation that guillotine clippers can cause, especially in larger breeds. If this is the case with your dog, try the pliers type and pick one that matches the size of your dog's nails.

Place your dog where you can easily reach his feet, either standing on a grooming table or counter, or sitting on the floor next to you. Position him where he can't pull away, then grasp his foot. Hold the clippers from behind the paw at about a 45-degree angle and snip firmly but quickly. Make sure the clipper is open fully again before moving to the next nail.

Just like your nails, your dog has a sensitive quick—a blood vessel that runs down the center of the nail, just short of the end. The quick is easily seen in mixes with light-colored nails. But with dark nails, it's a guessing game. Snip just a short amount from the end and work back. When you start seeing the layers (like lighter-

Grooming Table

A grooming table can make your grooming sessions much easier, particularly with medium- to larger-sized dogs. The surface is nonskid and water resistant, and the table folds for easy storage. Table options vary in height, so select one that allows you to easily reach your dog to comb, clip, or dry all his parts. Dogs learn to associate being placed on a table with grooming and realize that the appropriate behavior—standing or sitting still while being handled—is required during this time.

Attire and Accessories

Although your dog may not be as fashion-conscious as you are, he may still need a few items of doggy clothing. Mixes that are small or have short fur may need a sweater or coat during cold weather to keep them adequately warm. Dogs with very long facial fur stay cleaner if you use ribbons or a snood to pull their hair away from their food dish. And if you hike in rocky or overgrown terrain with your dog, a pair of boots may be advisable to keep his feet safe from injury.

colored circles) in the nail, stop—you are near the quick. If you accidentally nip your dog's quick, he'll likely yelp. Because the quick is blood-rich, you need to stop the bleeding. Don't make a huge fuss over your dog; apologize, stop the bleeding, and move on. Dip your dog's nail into a container of corn starch, apply a styptic stick, or use special bleed-stop powder made for dog nails.

Nails need to be trimmed every two weeks. Remember that the quick grows with the nail, and long nails have to be trimmed back slowly, cutting just a little at a time, maybe once a week until the quick recedes. If you're afraid of hurting your dog, ask your vet or groomer to cut them. For fun, apply some doggy nail polish if your dog enjoys pampering.

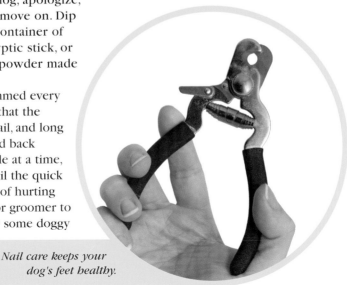

Nail care keeps your dog's feet healthy.

Chapter 5

Feeling Good

One way to ensure a long life with your dog is to provide him with regular quality healthcare. A qualified veterinarian, preventive medicine, and recognizing symptoms of illness in your dog are the basics for providing him a healthy life.

Finding a Veterinarian

To provide the best care for your dog, you need to find a knowledgeable, caring veterinarian. Because your dog's life depends on your vet's skill, don't cut corners by choosing the one with the least expensive fees— pick the clinic that offers the best quality care.

If you don't already have a vet you like, for convenience, look close to home or work first. But be willing to drive a distance if care is better elsewhere. Ask dog-owning neighbors and friends where they go and why they like a certain clinic. Dog trainers and groomers may also be a source for finding a veterinarian. Internet research can provide listings of veterinarians in your area.

Try to visit the animal clinic to see whether you would feel comfortable taking your dog there. Check to see whether it is clean and well run, and whether the staff is good with animals and their owners. Ask questions about the vet's experience and the clinic's policies and hours. If you get answers you don't like, or if the facility is dirty and disorganized, continue your search.

Keep in mind that your pet's health care is a team effort, so select a vet with whom you can talk easily. And trust your instincts: If you feel uneasy, so will your pet, so stick with a vet both you and your dog like.

Annual Vet Visits

The best way for your dog to stay healthy is to prevent problems or detect them early through an annual veterinary examination. When you first get your dog or puppy, take him to the vet for a thorough evaluation of his health. Then have him examined every year.

Annual veterinary checkups are necessar if you want your dog remain healthy.

A veterinary checkup is similar to what your physician does during your annual exam. Your dog's overall health is closely assessed by checking his weight, joints, and abdomen. The vet will listen to his heart and lungs, look closely at his ears, eyes, and mouth, and check the condition of his skin and fur.

A stool sample will be examined for worms, and your vet may draw blood to run tests that check the status of the liver, kidneys, and other organs. If your pet has existing health conditions, they will be monitored at this time; if necessary, other tests such as a urinalysis or x-rays may be done.

The annual exam is a good time to determine your dog's food and health plan for the upcoming year and to give vaccinations if they are due. Don't skip this step to good health. And as your dog advances in age, an exam every six months can help keep him healthier longer.

Vaccinations

Puppies are vaccinated (immunized against viruses) to prevent infection with deadly diseases. These shots are given two to three times over a period of several weeks. Vaccinations teach the body to recognize certain viruses and produce antibodies that kill them if your pup is exposed to a disease.

Adult dogs are given booster immunizations at varying periods throughout their lives. Vaccination schedules are currently being reevaluated by veterinarians because the practice of annual vaccination may be excessive. Despite these

FAMILY-FRIENDLY TIP

A Child's First Vet Visit

Any child that has been to a pediatrician can compare that experience with what your dog will undergo when he visits the veterinarian. Explain that although there may sometimes be discomfort, your dog will be healthier and will understand that you are taking good care of him.

changes, vaccination is essential to your dog's health. Discuss with your veterinarian how often your dog should be revaccinated.

Besides a schedule, you and your vet should determine which vaccines your dog needs. Not all dogs require all vaccines, depending on where you live and what activities you and your dog engage in.

The following are the most commonly administered vaccines.

Distemper

This deadly, highly contagious virus (usually spread through dog-to-dog contact) infects many organs and causes fever, nasal and eye discharge, dehydration, and hardening of the foot pads. Other respiratory and intestinal symptoms may also exist.

Most dogs die from this disease if infected. There is no treatment for distemper. Those that recover may be paralyzed or suffer other neurological complications. Immunization prevents infection. Shots are given between the ages of 8 and 16 weeks.

Infectious Canine Hepatitis

Although the liver is the primary target of hepatitis, the kidneys, lining of the blood vessels, and the eyes are also affected. Sick dogs may experience loss of appetite, high fever, vomiting, bloody diarrhea, and jaundice. Abdominal pain may cause a hunched posture, and the eyes can develop a blue cast similar to cataracts.

The virus is transmitted through infested urine, feces, saliva, and discharge from the eyes, and it sometimes can be fatal. Treatment is mostly supportive. Fluids may be given to prevent dehydration. Vaccinations are given between the ages of 8 and 12 weeks.

Kennel Cough (Bordetella)

Bordetellosis is not just one disease, but a group of diseases that cause upper respiratory illness. The main symptoms are a harsh cough and bronchitis. Coughing may be so severe, that your dog gags or retches.

The disease is quite contagious and can be spread when a dog coughs or sneezes. Infection can also occur if beds, bowls, or toys are shared. Dogs who are boarded in kennels or exposed

Vaccinations help protect your dog against disease.

to other dogs in places like dog parks or day cares are at greater risk of catching the disease.

Because kennel cough can be caused by multiple strains of the parainfluenza virus or bordetella bacteria, immunization may not prevent all kennel cough infections. But some boarding facilities may demand proof of bordetella vaccination. Your vet can recommend whether or not your dog should be immunized for the disease, either by shot or nasal spray, and whether he needs a booster.

In most cases no treatment is necessary. Cough suppressants may help, and antibiotics may be prescribed to prevent secondary infections for dogs who are at risk due to existing heart or respiratory disease.

Canine parainfluenza is considered part of the kennel cough complex, even though it is caused by a virus and not bacteria. Immunization normally is done as part of the bordetella vaccine.

Lyme Disease
Disease following a tick bite may result in a number of infections, including Lyme disease. Frequency of this bacterial infection is on the rise. However, not all dogs may be exposed to ticks or live where Lyme disease exists. Your veterinarian can advise you if your dog needs the Lyme vaccine.

If bitten and infected, your dog may experience fever, fatigue and loss of appetite, but the main symptoms are swollen, painful joints. Heart problems may also develop, as can chronic arthritis. Antibiotics, often long term, are used to kill the bacteria, and anti-inflammatories may be given to reduce pain and swelling.

Parvovirus
This difficult-to-kill virus is highly contagious, particularly to puppies.

The Expert Knows

Altering
Also known as spaying or neutering, altering your pet is one of the most important responsibilities an owner has. Altering is good for your dog's health, reducing or eliminating the possibility of several diseases. But there's another important reason to alter your pet. Although mixed-breed dogs are unique, there is likely never a good reason to have your mix reproduce. He may have come from a shelter or been taken in as a stray, and you have the ability to keep him from producing more homeless dogs. Remember, if you neuter your dog, you help reduce the number of animals euthanized because no one planned for or wanted them. Bringing a puppy into the world should only be done by knowledgeable breeders who try to improve the quality of a specific breed and by individuals willing to make a lifetime commitment to any puppies born.

Infection results in frequent and copious bouts of vomiting and diarrhea that is often bloody. Dehydration can occur quickly, with death following in as little as a few hours. Affected dogs are given fluids and drugs to reduce vomiting and diarrhea.

Infection is easily passed through contact with contaminated bowls, bedding, and toys, and the virus can even be carried on clothing or fur to other locations. Although parvovirus has mutated into new strains, vaccination can still provide immunity against most infections. Shots may be given between the ages of six and eight weeks, up through the age of about four or five months.

Rabies

Rabies is a fatal virus that infects the brain and nervous system of dogs bitten by another rabid animal, usually wildlife. Besides causing difficulty in drinking water, symptoms also include fever, itching, aggression or personality changes, paralysis, and eventually death. There is no treatment or cure.

Vaccination against rabies is required by law. Immunization is done first at age three or six months, then at one year. Revaccination is also mandated by law and may be required every three years, or annually, depending on your state.

Parasites

Just the thought of creepy crawlies on or inside your dog is enough to make most owners shudder. But parasites can cause disease, so the best defense is a good offense. Learn to recognize and treat— or when possible, prevent— infestation by fleas, ticks, worms, and more.

Internal Parasites

Mostly worms, internal parasites live primarily in the intestines. However, their changing life cycles cause some of them to end up in the heart, lung, or other organs.

Heartworms

As the name describes, these worms live in a dog's heart and the surrounding blood vessels. Infestation is acquired from the bite of mosquitoes infected with the microfilariae of the parasite. Heartworms go through various stages and life cycles, and they cause different problems along the way. Heartworm disease progresses rapidly, and by the time your dog shows symptoms the infestation may be extensive. Symptoms include coughing (possibly bloody), exercise intolerance, shortness of breath, weakness, fainting, and abnormal lung and heart sounds. Congestive heart failure, damage to the heart, and death may result.

A variety of preventives are available from your veterinarian. Some ingredients may cause severe reactions in Collie-type dogs, so if your mix is part Collie or Sheltie, be sure to let your vet know.

Have your dog tested each spring to be certain the preventive is working. If your dog does test positive for heartworms, treatment is available. However, prevention is far more effective since the medication used to kill the heartworms may also cause death or serious illness.

Heartworm preventive also prevents other common worms.

Hookworms

Found in soil and the feces of other animals, these tiny worms enter a dog's system, usually through the skin, or are passed from mother dog to puppy. The worms migrate to the intestine, where they "hook" onto the wall and feed.

Hookworms can cause anemia, bloody diarrhea, weakness, and weight loss. This parasite can be killed with appropriate deworming medicine but is more easily prevented.

Roundworms

This spaghetti-like parasite is the worm most commonly found in dogs. Even in spotless kennels, puppies are usually born with roundworms and are dewormed when very young.

Roundworms contaminate soil and live in feces from infected animals. If an adult dog is exposed to these

Tapeworms

Dogs acquire tapeworms primarily from swallowing fleas that are hosts to the worms' larvae. Once in the dog, the larvae develop into worms and attach to the intestine. Tapeworms grow by segments, with each segment reproducing itself. Because of this, tapeworm infestations can become massive quickly.

The first sign usually noticed is the presence of tiny, mobile, rice-like pieces near your dog's anus or in his stools. Weight loss, reduced appetite, and diarrhea are also possible. A medication specific to tapeworms is necessary to kill this parasite. To prevent tapeworms, prevent fleas from getting on your dog, and don't let him catch and eat small wildlife.

Whipworms

Another worm named for its appearance, whipworms live in the soil. Dogs get infested if they ingest dirt that contains the worm's eggs. Although they grow to about 2 inches (5 cm), whipworms may not always be present in tested stool samples.

Symptoms that your dog might have whipworms are diarrhea, weight loss, sluggishness, and a sick-looking appearance. Multiple treatments may be needed to eradicate the worm, but like other worms, they are preventable.

Should You Insure Your Pet?

Health insurance is available for pets too. Just as it is for people, high-tech treatment is available for your dog, but costs can be high. If a pet policy covers these options, and you don't want to take a chance on not being covered, get quotes from different companies and buy a policy. Fees and coverage vary, and policies may have exclusions for certain types of care. If your budget can't support extensive pet insurance, consider making regular deposits to a savings account to be used for emergency pet care only.

contaminated substances, roundworm infestation may occur. Like most other worms, the roundworm migrates through the body as its life cycle progresses.

If your dog has a pot belly, a gagging cough with retching, vomits, and is lethargic, roundworms may be present. With a heavy infestation, a dog may vomit or pass live worms. Prevention is the same as for hookworms, but deworming requires multiple treatments.

External Parasites

Parasites that live on the outside of your dog have the potential not only to make him itchy but also to cause serious disease. And these pests can pester humans as well. Keep your dog's area clean and debris-free to help reduce or eliminate fleas, ticks, and mites.

Fleas

When your dog goes outside, he's at risk for getting fleas. These hopping pests feed on blood and don't care if it comes from a dog, cat, or a human. They multiply rapidly and in a very short time can rule not only your yard and your pet's fur, but your carpet, furniture, and bedding as well.

Some dogs have allergic reactions to flea bites, and fleas transmit tapeworms. They make life itchy and miserable for everyone. Although fleas are not entirely preventable outdoors, you can eliminate or prevent their existence on your dog and in your home.

Flea preventives for your dog are available in a variety of forms,

Always check your dog for ticks, mites, and fleas after he's been playing outdoors.

as are pesticides for your house and yard. These are potent products and can cause bad reactions, even death, if used improperly. It's important to use them exactly as directed, for as long as needed, in order to kill all fleas and eggs.

Be sure to wash bedding, toys, and grooming tools too. All dogs must be treated, possibly with a flea bath or powder, prior to being given a preventive. It's easier to prevent fleas than eradicate them: Keep your dog's outdoor area mowed, your carpets vacuumed, and your dog on a preventive.

Mites

If no fleas are evident and your dog is scratching vigorously and losing fur, he may be afflicted with mites. Mites cause a condition commonly referred to as mange. There are three types of mites that cause differing conditions, but all cause discomfort and similar signs such as oozing, scabbed, or damaged skin.

Dirty living conditions can promote some mites, and the scabies type is contagious. Demodecosis may be inherited. All mange must be treated by a veterinarian, usually with a topical insecticide. Medications may be given to reduce itching or to prevent infection.

Ticks

Ticks are like vampires: they are blood-sucking arachnids that attach to your dog and drink his blood until full. They may live on your dog for several days, laying eggs while they're there.

Although not as annoying as fleas, ticks are far more dangerous because they can infect your dog with Lyme disease, Rocky Mountain spotted fever, ehrlichiosis, or babesiosis. These diseases are serious, potentially fatal, and difficult to diagnose and treat.

It's best to keep your dog safe by preventing ticks from biting him. Keep his outdoor play area clean of high weeds and brushy undergrowth. Use a preventive recommended by your vet, and brush or bathe him thoroughly after exposure to natural tick habitats.

If you find a tick on your dog, remove it carefully but firmly with a pair of tweezers, then cleanse the bite and surrounding skin with alcohol. Watch him during the following days and report symptoms to your vet if your dog becomes ill.

Common Health Issues in Dogs

All dogs, no matter how healthy, get sick sometimes. Here are a few of the more common problems your mix may experience.

Allergies

If your dog's mix includes a breed prone to allergies, he's more likely to develop them. But don't expect him to sniffle and sneeze. Although respiratory and eye symptoms can occur in dogs, canine allergies more often manifest themselves in the skin, causing intense itching, flaking, or rashes. The ears may be involved, resulting in itching and the production of more wax.

Dogs tend to be most allergic to certain foods, such as grains or meat proteins. Allergens like pollen and grass or cleansers and detergents all can cause problems.

The severity of your dog's reaction will determine the treatment. But be prepared to change his food, his bedding, or your laundry detergent to reduce flare-ups.

Cancer

Like humans, dogs can get many kinds of cancer. Certain breeds have a disposition to specific types, and if your mix includes these breeds, it's important to learn the warning signs. When caught early, many cancers are treatable.

Owners may notice a fast-growing or unusual lump or bump. Other symptoms can include abnormal bleeding, sudden weight loss, fatigue, loss of appetite, pain, or a foul odor. Malignant growths can occur in just about every organ or tissue, including bone, skin, lungs, liver, stomach, and lymph glands.

If your dog's habits change or you notice a new swelling, have him examined by a vet. Tissue can be checked for malignancy, and if positive, the same treatment options—surgery, chemotherapy, radiation, and more—available for people are also offered to dogs by veterinary oncologists.

Cataracts

Often as a part of aging or an inherited condition, dogs may develop cataracts. Diabetes or an eye injury can also cause them.

Cataracts cause the lens of the eye to become opaque, with a whitish-bluish cast. As light is blocked, vision is lost. Owners may not notice a cataract until it's large enough to have already caused vision loss. There are usually no other symptoms, except when a dog seems not to notice motion in his range of sight.

Surgery by a veterinary ophthalmologist is possible to remove cataracts, especially in a young dog. As with human cataract surgery, a new lens can be implanted if the cataract is not too extensive.

Dental Issues

Is your mixed breed toy-sized? If so, he could have retained baby teeth. This occurs when a permanent tooth fails to push out the baby tooth. Retained teeth need to be removed by a veterinarian.

SENIOR DOG TIP

Coping With a Senior's Declining Health

The age at which your mix becomes a senior will depend on what breeds he has in his background. For example, smaller dogs such as terriers tend to be longer lived than some very large breeds like Great Danes and Bullmastiffs.

As with people, older dogs develop age-related health problems and body parts begin to fail. Watch for signs of disease and seek veterinary care when new symptoms arise. Checkups twice a year are a good way to ensure your senior remains healthy.

Along with proper health care, consider daily quality of life issues. Make your senior's environment comfortable and cozy. And be sure to keep his mind active, which can help prevent senility. He may sleep more and play less, but will love you just the same. Be patient and kind with your old pal. He was always there for you as a youngster; be there for him now when he needs you more.

65

Feeling Good

Brachycephalic (short, flattened muzzle) mixes can have problems with misaligned teeth. Teeth that are not properly aligned can cause chewing problems and pain. Food can get caught between the teeth, making them susceptible to decay. Crooked teeth can be removed, or veterinary specialists similar to orthodontists can apply devices to straighten them.

All dogs can develop gingivitis or periodontal disease. Without proper dental care, food that remains on the teeth after eating causes buildup of plaque and tartar. This buildup leads to inflammation and tenderness of the gums. Eventually, teeth decay, the gums recede, and pus forms in pockets around affected teeth. These conditions are preventable with regular brushing and periodic veterinary cleanings.

Ear Infections

Dogs with drop (pendulous) ears and those with heavy fur growth in the ears are more prone to ear infections. Dogs with food sensitivities, such as to soy, may also have more frequent ear problems.

Signs that your dog might have otitis (inflammation or infection of the ear) include scratching at the head or ears, pain when touched on the head, head shaking, or bad odor. Your vet may prescribe antibiotics or drying agents to put directly into the ear. Regular careful cleaning can reduce the

Knowing how to recognize potential health problems and how to handle them is important to your dog' overall well-being.

likelihood of infections, as can finding the best diet for your dog.

Epilepsy

Epilepsy is a neurological condition that results in seizures. Seizures cause a dog to become rigid, collapse, have uncontrollable tremors or movement of the legs and feet, foam from the mouth or drool, or appear to lose consciousness. He may also lose control of his bladder or bowels. Personality or behavior changes may occur before or after the episode, and your dog may be disoriented.

Seizures result when nerve signals misfire in the brain and can be caused by an undetermined problem within the brain itself. They can also be the result of a head injury, low blood sugar, exposure to toxins, or other disease processes. Medications are used to control this life-long condition.

Hypothyroidism

An insufficiency of thyroid hormone is a common problem in all types of dogs. Many of the body's organs and systems are affected by this condition, so symptoms vary from dog to dog. Typical signs are weight gain, thin fur, dry or scaly skin, bulging eyes, cold intolerance, personality change, and lethargy.

Diagnosis is made by testing the blood for thyroid hormone. Untreated disease can result in organ damage or death, but hypothyroidism is easily treated with a daily tablet of the missing hormone. Periodic blood tests are necessary to check the level of

Holistic Veterinarians

Holistic care encompasses treatment of the whole dog—it takes into account his physical, emotional, and behavioral well-being. A holistic veterinarian combines conventional and alternative therapies for a treatment plan that is the most effective but the least harmful or painful for the dog.

thyroid hormone once your dog is on medication.

Orthopedic Conditions

Probably the most common orthopedic problems seen in dogs are hip dysplasia and patellar luxation. Both conditions tend to be inherited and appear more often in certain breeds. You may not know whether your mixed-breed dog is at risk. If he's a large dog, he may be more likely to have hip dysplasia, and if he is small, he might be at risk for luxating patellas.

Hip dysplasia is a condition where the hip bone develops without a socket into which the thigh bone can fit and move correctly. Dogs with dysplasia often bunny hop when running or have difficulty climbing

First Aid for Your Dog

Know the basics of first aid in case your dog needs care before a veterinarian can be reached. Being prepared for an emergency can make the difference between life and death. Keep supplies in a kit that is easily located. Your first aid kit should include:

- bandages
- elastic bandage or vet wrap
- nonstick gauze pads and tape
- cotton balls and swabs
- alcohol
- antibiotic cream
- hydrogen peroxide
- saline solution
- instant ice pack
- scissors
- tweezers
- thermometer
- antihistamine
- antiemetic
- ipecac syrup
- antidiarrheal
- muzzle
- blanket and towels
- canine first-aid manual
- a complete list of your dog's medications

If you think your pet has been poisoned, call your vet or the ASPCA National Animal Poison Control Center at (888) 426-4435 immediately; an expert will be available to help you 24 hours a day, 365 days a year. A consultation fee may be billed to your credit card.

Some American Red Cross offices teach pet first aid. To find out whether there's one in your area, go to www.redcross.org. Or ask your vet for a referral.

There are many alternative health care options that work with conventional medicine.

stairs. Eventually, arthritis develops in the joint and movement becomes difficult and painful. Replacement surgery is available but can be costly and have an extensive recuperative period.

Patellar luxation is a long name for a slipped kneecap. Although it doesn't sound serious, this condition can range from simple to crippling. The signs usually appear in young adulthood, with an affected dog skipping or stretching a leg out behind himself while walking. Mild conditions require no treatment, but worsening luxation needs surgical correction.

Weight loss can help with both conditions, as can anti-inflammatory drugs prescribed by your vet.

Alternative Therapies

Besides traditional medical care, your veterinarian may be able to offer you some alternative care options. These therapies have been practiced throughout the world for many centuries and may be useful in some chronic or terminal conditions.

Ask your vet whether alternative therapy may be less painful or stressful and can help your dog's health. Options include acupuncture, chiropractic, homeopathy, herbs and supplements, massage, and even energy healing.

Chapter 6

Being Good

You want your dog to be a good dog—well mannered, obedient, observant of household rules—and you want him to respond to your direction. Teaching your puppy or rescue dog how to become a well-adjusted member of the family goes beyond feeding and housetraining. Training is work that you do in simple ways every day to teach basic manners. It is also work you do for a period of time in a concentrated, organized setting to teach obedience skills. The earlier you begin, the better off your dog, and your relationship with him, will be for a lifetime.

Training will not only help your dog fit into your family routine but will also enable him to feel secure because he will know what is expected of him.

Reasons to Train

Dogs learn quickly. They can learn new behaviors almost daily—including how to break household rules and not get caught! It's easier to train for good behavior from the beginning than it is to untrain bad habits later. Whether your mix is a pup, an adult, or a senior, it's up to you to teach him appropriate behavior because he doesn't know what's expected of him in your home unless you tell him. Your family is your dog's pack, and packs have a structure of authority with you as the leader, which your dog must learn to follow. Although some dogs may want to be in charge, your mix shouldn't run the household. He will look to you for direction on how to behave, and it is your responsibility to set boundaries. His security and happiness depend on it.

To train your dog successfully, it's also essential to learn about canine behavior because it will help you understand not only how to work with him, but why he behaves the way he does. Knowing what your dog is saying through his body language and vocalizations, as well as how your own body language and tone affect him, can be very helpful during the training process. Clear communication is the key to effective training. As an added benefit, the interaction that occurs between you and your dog during training forms a close bond to develop between you.

If you attend a formal class, you'll be taught how to get your dog's attention and how to best train him. In a class setting, a dog learns how to adapt to new situations and different environments, plus he meets many new people and dogs.

However you decide to train your mix, determine the rules and abide by them. Make sure they are reasonable and fair. Then be consistent in when, where, and how you enforce them, and make sure every member of your family understands and follows them too.

Socialization

Dogs are social animals. They need to be around people and, often, other animals. Socialization is the word used to describe the process of teaching your dog how to behave around strangers and other animals, and how to feel comfortable and confident in new places. Without socialization, your dog could become fearful, timid, or aggressively protective of his territory or possessions.

Because mixed-breed dogs are often rescues and adopted as adults, they may not have been socialized. Or they may have come from an abusive situation. If so, socialization is particularly important—it can give your dog the confidence to overcome his fears.

How to Socialize Your Dog

Expose your dog to a wide variety of people, animals, places, sounds, smells, and objects in a positive but controlled manner. Always have him on leash, for his safety and that of others. Begin the process slowly by introducing him to one new situation at a time in a familiar environment. Avoid anything that may cause undue stress or fear. Explain to your dog what's going to happen, whom he'll be meeting, where you're going, or what he'll be doing. Tell him how you expect him to behave.

Calmly introduce your dog to the new place, person, or animal as if the situation is routine. If your dog acts hyper, teach him to "settle." If he's afraid, calm him by telling him everything is alright. Let him see that the situation is nonthreatening. Don't force him to investigate, but don't remove him right away either.

When he appears to be confident with this, try taking a short trip to a new environment, such as a drive-through window (where your dog will probably get a treat!) or on a walk up the street to meet a neighbor. Your dog will be better behaved, more flexible, and confident if properly socialized.

The Expert Knows

Watch Your Language!

Dogs are masters at understanding us, even when we don't say a word. They read our body posture and the tone of our voice to detect our moods. Sometimes, however, our body language communicates a different message from what we're verbally saying to our dogs. Avoid confusion by knowing exactly what you want your dog to do—and not do—and communicate that clearly to him, both verbally and physically. Give him only one command at a time, and be consistent when and how you issue the command.

Crate Training

Dogs need a space to call their own, and a crate serves this function. Also, until your puppy is reliably housetrained and no longer chews on off-limit items, his crate is the safest place for him to be while you're busy or away. But his crate is not a substitute for supervision, nor is it a doggy jail. Your dog should not be left in his crate more than four hours at a time, and no longer than eight or nine hours during the day. Use your dog's crate wisely and it will be a good training tool for you and a safe place for him.

How to Crate Train Your Dog

Have your dog's crate waiting upon his arrival. Place it where it will be out of the way of hectic activity, but where he can see or hear you. At first, you may want to situate his crate in your bedroom so he doesn't feel alone at night.

You may need to persuade your dog to enter his crate for the first time. Put a few treats in the back of the crate. Allow him to explore it and come out on his own. To make the crate a place he wants to be, leave a few safe toys inside. Also try feeding him in his crate.

Once he's seems comfortable with the crate, you may want your dog to learn to enter it on command. Teach him a phrase like "get in your crate." When he enters on his own, praise him and give him a favorite treat or toy. If your dog whines or barks continuously to get out before it's

Exposure to new people, places, and experiences will help ensure that your dog is friendly, flexible, and confident in any situation.

time, tap your finger against the front of his crate and tell him "settle." Praise him when he quiets down. Eventually, his crate should become your dog's favorite space.

Housetraining

The most important behavior you teach your dog is making sure he eliminates outside only. Housetraining is time consuming, but it's essential not to skip any steps. If you're reliable in your training, your dog will be reliable in his housetraining.

How to Housetrain Your Dog

The first time you bring your new dog home, immediately take him to the outdoor area where you want him to eliminate. When he does, praise him, then take him inside and allow him to remain out of his crate. If he doesn't go, take him inside and place him into his crate. Although puppies don't have much control, all dogs are born with the instinct to keep their "den" clean. Placing your dog into his crate trains him to wait until he's outdoors to eliminate.

Remember that puppies need to eliminate frequently, as may an untrained adult dog. Shortly after eating, drinking, sleeping, or playing, puppies will need to go out. Adults that need housetraining should be put out on the same schedule. Try to take your new dog out every two or three hours while he's learning.

When you take your dog outside, urge him to "go potty." Don't engage in play until he has eliminated. When he

Signs Your Dog Needs to Go Out

Puppies may not give much notice that they're about to urinate, but there are some telltale signs that can offer some warning. Watch for circling, sniffing the floor, sudden frantic activity, walking back and forth, or loss of attention to play. Your pup may also begin to squat or sit, or go to the door and whimper. If you notice any of these signs, take him out immediately.

Indications that your pup needs to empty his bowels come on more slowly and may be more obvious. He may walk back and forth in a pattern, intently sniffing the floor as the size of the area he walks decreases. He may pass gas, look at his stomach, or get into a humped-over squat. If he doesn't defecate while he's out to urinate, and he later engages in one of these actions, return him to his outdoor potty zone.

does, praise him enthusiastically. A slow learner can be encouraged by being rewarded immediately with a treat.

When housetraining your dog, choose a spot in your yard where you want him to eliminate and take him to that same area every time

Before you put your dog into his crate for the night, take him out again. When he empties his bladder or bowels, praise him and bring him inside. Allow him a few more minutes with you before placing him into his crate. Otherwise, you'll be sending a mixed message about why he's being crated. Pottying outdoors earns your dog cuddle and play time out of his crate. If he doesn't go while out, place him back into his crate and try again in a few minutes. He'll soon learn to associate eliminating outside with crate-free time with you.

Until your dog is fully housetrained, don't let him out of your sight. Keep him in one room with you. As he learns to eliminate outdoors, allow his indoor area to expand, but still watch him. Eventually, he'll learn that the entire house is his den and that he may not eliminate anywhere inside it.

Be consistent when and how you housetrain your pup. Changing the routine results in confusion and accidents. But even if you do everything right, there will still be times during the housetraining process when your dog has an accident. Reasons may be that he is sick or you're unable to make it home in time. When an accident happens, do not punish your dog. Take him outside, clean up the mess thoroughly so no odor remains that your dog can detect, and praise him when he eliminates outdoors. Your dog needs to understand that the location where he eliminated is wrong, not that he was bad.

Basic Commands

Formal training is a good way for you and your dog to become a team. Whether in class or at home, teaching your dog basic obedience commands exercises his brain and body, making him a smarter, healthier dog. It provides him with guidance and security. You both learn to communicate with each other, and it deepens the bond you share.

Basic obedience is the foundation for all formal training and begins with the *sit, down, stay, come,* and *heel* commands. Each mix has a personality all his own, based partly on the different breed qualities he's inherited. A good trainer can help you determine how to fine tune your training techniques to elicit your dog's best response.

Before starting on the basic commands, teach your dog to watch you—if you don't have his attention he won't learn. With your dog in front of you, hold a treat or toy near your mouth and say "watch me." When you have his full attention, give him his reward. Once he learns to watch you on command, begin teaching the basics.

Keep training sessions short—about 15 to 30 minutes—and stop after your dog has done a command well. Practice your work together several times a week.

Sit

The *sit* command puts your dog into a calm or safe position. It helps you to teach him to wait patiently while you put his food bowl down, put on his leash, or get him ready to load into your car, as well many other daily activities.

How to Teach Sit

With your dog in front of you, hold a treat above his head and move it back and down while saying the word "sit." Your dog should automatically sit as he follows the treat.

If he moves backwards instead of sitting, try guiding him into a seated position by either gently sliding your

FAMILY-FRIENDLY TIP

Kids, K9s, and Training

If your child is mature, responsible, and physically strong enough, or is the primary person with whom your dog spends time, why not let her be the one to train your dog? Of course, you should supervise all training sessions and be involved by helping with fees, books, transportation, and support.

You can interest young children in dog training by allowing them to hand you your dog's reward treats. They can also participate by offering praise to your dog when you do. While your dog is learning to behave, they will learn responsible care for an animal.

Basic obedience commands like the sit-stay are the foundation for good manners and all future learning.

hand down his back or curving your hand under his rear legs. For smaller mixes, you may want to sit on the floor when teaching this command.

When your dog sits, say "good boy, good sit." If he jumps back up immediately, try again. Give him the treat after he remains seated for a few seconds. Practice until he associates sitting with receiving a reward, and then until he responds without the treat held above his head. Eventually, your dog will learn to sit just receiving verbal praise.

Down

The *down* command places your dog into a prone position on the floor, with his rear legs beneath him and his forelegs stretched out in front of his body. A dog in *down* does not lie over on his side but is ready to get up on command.

Down is useful for keeping your dog in a more comfortable position for a longer period of time, such as when he's waiting in the veterinarian's lobby. A strong-willed dog may resist this command because it places him into a submissive position. But praise and rewards will get your dog to learn the *down* in a short time.

Don't confuse *down* with *off*. Use the *off* command when you want your dog to get off the counter or furniture. Use *down* when you want him to lie down. Don't combine the *sit* and the *down* commands either; use one or the other so your dog is not confused about which action you want him to perform.

How to Teach Down

Begin teaching this command from the sit position. From there, your dog is halfway to down. If your mix is small, it might help to kneel next to him while teaching this command.

Take a treat or toy and slowly lower it to the floor in front of your dog while saying "down." If your dog starts to stand or doesn't drop, lay your other hand on the middle of his back without applying pressure. As he starts to crouch, move the treat slightly forward so that he must slide into a full lying down position to reach it.

When your dog is down, say "good boy, good down" and give him a reward. Do not ask him to stay in the *down* position very long while he's first learning the command. With each practice session, have your dog remain in *down* a little longer.

Eventually, teach your dog to perform the *down* while you're standing beside him. He should also learn to respond to the command from a standing position.

Stay

The *stay* command is nearly always used with the *sit* or *down* command. It's useful when you need your dog to hold a position for awhile, such as when he's being groomed. Your dog may learn *stay* more easily from the *sit*

position first, particularly if he does not like doing a *down*.

How to Teach Stay

Have your dog sit at your left side. Use a firm, low voice that goes down in pitch (think of how a motor sounds winding down to a stop). Say "s-t-a-y" so it sounds long. While telling him to stay, put your left arm slightly up and in front of you. Open your hand, palm facing your dog, and move it toward his face. Moving your arm up and down once, simulating a barrier he can't cross, may also be helpful.

Starting with your right foot (another signal to your dog not to move), slowly take two steps away from your dog. Then turn and face him. Wait only a few seconds, return to his side, and say "good stay, good boy."

If your dog gets up before you return to his side, get his attention with a clucking sound, gently guide

Training Treats

It is essential to reward your dog quickly after a correct response during training. To make this possible, offer treats that are small and soft. Avoid hard or large, crumbly biscuits or raw vegetables. Try commercial training treats, semi-moist treats, little bites of cheese, or dried cooked liver. Don't give a training treat unless your dog earns it. For big breakthroughs, though, you can offer a jackpot—lots of treats at once.

him back into position, and begin again. While he's still learning, you can hold the hand signal and repeat the command until he understands what you want him to do.

Once he successfully obeys the command, release him from his stay with an enthusiastic "ok" and reward him with a treat, toy, or snuggle.

Come

The most practical command you can teach your dog is to come when you call him. For example, if he's outdoors he should be ready to come inside as soon as you call. Most importantly, if your dog ever gets away from you, calling him to come could save his life.

How to Teach Come

Your dog needs to learn that good things happen when he comes to you. Never call him to come if you are going to punish him or do something to him he dislikes, such as giving him medicine. That teaches him to be afraid to come.

Begin by walking your dog on a long leash. At first, keep the leash short, then let some length out and walk briskly backwards while calling your dog to come. Say "come" along with his name, and use a high-pitched, excited voice. As your dog comes toward you, gather up the extra leash in your hands so he can't run past you. Praise him enthusiastically, tell him "good boy, good come" and give him his favorite reward.

While he's still learning, don't tell

Hitting Isn't Training

Hitting a dog is never appropriate. Hitting is punishment, which dogs do not understand. If you hit your dog, the only message he receives is to be afraid of you or whatever you use to hit him.

If your dog is behaving inappropriately, try to understand what he is thinking as a dog— what he is doing may be natural behavior for a canine. To correct your dog properly, first get his attention by interrupting him with a "no." Then show him an acceptable behavior instead. Offer praise when he responds correctly.

your dog to come unless you are able to enforce the command. A good way to teach your dog that the *come* command is fun is to use it to call him for his dinner.

Heel

Heeling is when your dog walks calmly beside you on your left side. It's a command that makes walking your dog easier and more pleasant for you and those you encounter on your outings.

When training is a positive experience, most dogs can learn everything they need to know.

How to Teach Heel

Have your dog sit at your left side on leash. Start walking, always stepping off with your left foot first. This becomes a signal to your dog that you're about to move and he should walk beside you. Say "heel" as you begin walking.

Don't get into a tug of war. If your dog doesn't get up and walk with you, or if he lags behind, coax him by holding a treat down by your side where he should be walking. While learning, repeat the *heel* command whenever you want your dog to return to your side.

If your dog pulls on the leash, gently shorten the length of leash he has available, and draw him back to you. Keep walking and say "heel" again. You can slip the leash around your back

if he continues to pull. This makes it impossible for your dog to get ahead of you. Just be careful not to shorten the leash so much that you strain your dog's neck or step on him.

When your dog walks calmly beside you, praise him by saying "good boy, good heel." As he learns to heel automatically, you should limit the use of the command when you begin walking.

Leash Training

Start with getting your puppy used to a collar—a nylon one with a break-away buckle usually works best. Select a size that is slightly larger than your puppy's neck and adjust it so that you can easily slip three to four fingers beneath it. Make certain to adjust it as your puppy grows. A few dogs will scratch

Finding a Professional Trainer

For professional obedience training, find an instructor who is right for your dog's personality. For example, a loud, forceful trainer won't work if your dog is timid. Your breeder, veterinarian, or local groomer may provide reliable recommendations, or you can contact the Association of Pet Dog Trainers at (800) PET-DOGS or search their website at www.apdt.com for the name of a trainer near you. You can also ask your dog-owning friends and neighbors where they trained their dogs.

Before enrolling in a class, visit a session and make sure that it is well organized, uses positive training methods, and that both the dogs and owners look relaxed.

- Here are some questions you should ask:
- What kind of training methods do you use?
- How do you handle training problems?
- How long are the training sessions?
- What kind of experience and credentials do you have?

The expert instruction and advice of a professional trainer can teach you how to understand your dog better, how to communicate with him more effectively, and how to solve training problems that might be difficult for you to resolve on your own.

or attempt to bite at a collar when you first put it on them, but most quickly forget its presence as soon as feeding or play time begins.

For walking your mix, choose a leash that is long enough to easily reach his level without you having to stretch or pull on his neck. The material should be durable but not heavy, and the leash should be comfortable for you to hold in your hand.

Start indoors, and let your puppy smell the leash then clip it to his collar. One method is to let your puppy drag the leash around on the floor while you supervise. As he adapts to its presence you pick it up, and with a treat entice him to come to you.

Another technique is to show the puppy that through the leash you are connected to each other. When he walks around you follow him. This will get his attention. As he watches you walking with him, show him a treat and walk away from him, still holding the leash and enticing him to now follow you and the treat you are holding. Praise and offer treats as he continues to follow you around. Eventually, take him outside and repeat

SENIOR DOG TIP

Training Older Dogs

Learning something new helps keep an older dog physically and mentally active, which is good for him. Just remember, when training your senior:

- be patient
- go slowly
- offer enthusiastic praise
- don't try to teach a command that his old body no longer allows him to do

the procedure. Soon he will learn that his leash is associated with pleasant activities like outings.

If your mix has tracheal problems, or has had neck, back, or spinal injuries, he may be more comfortable walking on leash with a harness instead of a collar.

Chapter **7**

In the

Doghouse

All dogs are good dogs. Humans don't always
see it that way, though. Normal behaviors for a
dog—barking, digging, chewing—are perceived
as problematic if they occur excessively or in the
wrong places. Like people, dogs aren't perfect, but
they try to please; most can be taught to adapt
their behavior to live with us.

Undesirable behaviors often arise out of boredom and lack of sufficient exercise. Providing your dog with outlets for his energy, toys, and plenty of attention can help prevent most common problems.

Problem Behaviors

When your dog destroys your shoes, barks endlessly at nothing, or does something else that displeases you, he's not trying to make you angry, he's just being a dog. Dogs don't intentionally engage in spiteful or destructive behavior. Whatever they do, they have a doggy reason; we just may not understand it.

Before you get upset with your dog, ask yourself why he's behaving the way he is. The answer will usually be that he's following his instincts: alerting, hunting, playing, or relieving boredom or anxiety. Don't punish your dog, and don't give up on him by turning him over to a shelter. Have patience, work with him, and show him an acceptable way to redirect his drive and energy.

Biting and Nipping

Dog play, particularly between puppies, involves nipping, mouthing, gnawing, and gently biting each other. Mixes that are part herding-type dogs (Sheltie, Corgi) use their teeth when they work. However normal this behavior may be in certain situations, it's not acceptable for your dog to use his teeth on people.

If your dog nips any part of you, let him know it is inappropriate by loudly saying "ouch." Then turn away and ignore him. A dog that continues to nip during play should also be told firmly, "no bite," and placed into his crate with a chew toy. This teaches him that touching people with his teeth ends his play time.

Snarling or snapping are warnings that a dog may bite. Neither snapping nor biting should be allowed. A dog who bites is dangerous. Most often snapping or biting is a sign of a fearful, aggressive, or very dominant dog, and professional help, like that of a behaviorist or qualified trainer, should be sought. Even though a tiny dog may seem funny when he nips, growls, or bites, don't laugh at him. This encourages the behavior. Nipping shouldn't be ignored. Stop the behavior before your nipper becomes a nuisance. The exception to the rule: Your dog is allowed to bite in self-defense if he or your family is truly being attacked.

If your mix was adopted as an adult, his background may be unknown. A puppy that was removed from his mother too early may not have learned not to bite. A history of harsh training methods or abuse could cause an otherwise good-natured dog to bite. It is possible to teach your dog not to bite with a consistent, long-term effort and professional training.

If your well-behaved dog suddenly starts biting, consult a veterinarian immediately. He may be ill or injured.

Chewing

Puppies need to chew (or gnaw) as they teethe. Most dogs enjoy a good chew throughout their lives. Chewing and mouthing objects is also a way that dogs explore the world, deal with stress, or pass the time. There's no problem with chewing unless your dog's eating your socks or sofa.

FAMILY-FRIENDLY TIP

Always Supervise Children and Dogs

Dogs—even when well behaved and well trained—should always be supervised when they're with children. And children, especially young ones, need to be taught how to respect and properly handle a dog. Doing the following can help prevent problems:

- Never let your child poke, pull, grab, or otherwise mishandle your dog, who may resort to biting to defend himself.
- Teach your dog to be calm around your child.
- When you're trying to correct a problem behavior, such as chewing, explain to your children how you are training your dog to behave differently, and see that they interact with him in the same manner.
- If your dog has a serious issue, like aggression, keep children out of harm's way and seek professional advice on how to proceed.

To keep your possessions safe from a puppy's teeth, prevent him from chewing them in the first place. Supervise your pup whenever he's out of his crate, particularly when he's teething. An adult who's a big chewer needs to be watched until he learns what's alright to chew and what's off limits.

Make it a rule that if an object is on the floor it's alright for your dog to chew it. This means you must keep everything else—the remote, toys, clothing, papers—picked up. If you can't remove an item, like a chair, place a drop of bitter spray, vinegar, or lemon juice on the area where your dog tries to chew.

When you catch your dog starting to chew inappropriately, say "no chew." Take the object away from him (teach him to give you whatever he has when you ask) and immediately hand him one of his toys instead. Praise him when he takes it. Your dog will learn that only his toys are okay to chew and all other items—even if they're on the floor—are not. Provide him with plenty of safe toys that he can chew and that are always available.

Digging

If your mix is part terrier or retriever, he'll probably love to dig. Dogs dig because it's fun to unearth critters and bugs. It also helps pass the time if they're bored. The best way to stop your dog from digging is to provide him with an alternative activity that is as much fun.

Fill the holes your dog digs with large rocks or other objects he can't unearth. Then provide a small sandbox and bury toys in the sand, or allow him a corner of the yard where he is allowed to dig. Supervise his outdoor playtime and when he starts digging, tell him "no dig," and move him to his permissible dig zone. Point and say "here, dig" or "play here."

Terrier types may not be deterred from doing their job, which is digging up and catching underground prey.

If your dog chews something he shouldn't, immediately replace it with an appropriate chew toy.

If having a dog doesn't keep the wildlife out of your yard, thank your dog for doing his job—not for digging a hole—and tell him "enough." Fill the burrow and move him to his dig area. Likewise, Nordic types like to make earthen beds by digging indentations, particularly in extreme temperatures. Tell your dog "no dig," and provide a weatherproof bed on your deck or patio. Or, if one bed-hole is acceptable, place the bed there. Offer praise when your dog stops digging.

The Expert Knows

When to Seek Professional Help: Aggression and Domnance

If your dog is acting aggressively, this is a serious problem; he could injure your family, a guest, or another pet. Aggressive behavior includes snarling, growling, guarding, lunging, snapping at, and biting other dogs or pets and people. At least ten different types of aggression occur in dogs, with causes ranging from fear, protection of territory or possessions, to dominance.

Dominance and aggression are two different behaviors, but an overly dominant dog—one who insists on being head of the pack or household—can become aggressive if not trained properly. While it's normal for a group of dogs to have a leadership structure amongst themselves, aggressive behavior should resolve once the leader of the pack is established. Learn to distinguish the difference when your dogs are working out pack status.

Aggression never gets better on its own and can worsen as time passes. Enforce household rules in a firm but nonpunitive manner, and seek professional help immediately.

Excessive Barking

People talk, dogs bark; it's how they communicate. Certain types of mixes (Beagles, Schnauzers) talk more than others. Some barking is good. It's when it's too frequent or lasts too long that barking becomes a problem.

If your dog barks excessively, first figure out why he is barking. Is he telling you about visitors or strangers on your property? Are there other animals in his yard? Does he need water or to go out? Is he lonely or bored?

Once you understand why he's barking, thank him for telling you (for instance, if a guest is at your door), then tell him, "enough." Some dogs may get the idea to be quiet if you put your fingers to your lips and in a whisper say "sshhh, quiet," also.

Putting a dog outside to stop his barking doesn't work—it makes him bark more. When problem barking occurs outdoors, teach your dog to come when called and reward him with a treat. Keep him inside for several minutes until he quiets down. He'll soon learn he has to stop playing and come inside when he barks too much.

Yelling "enough" from the house may work if he's already learned the command. Another way to control barking by command is to teach your dog to "speak." Say "speak" and reward him with a treat and praise if he barks. Or set up a situation so that he barks when you say "speak." Once he's learned to speak on command, do the reverse. Tell him, "no bark," when he's quiet and praise him for quieting. You can also say "good quiet" when he's being quiet, then praise and offer a treat.

A fearful dog who barks frequently, or one who barks continually while you're away, has issues other than just talking too much. Ask your vet or trainer for help with dealing with your dog's fears. Once he learns he's safe, the barking should subside.

Even if you love the sound of your dog's voice, your neighbors may not. A quiet dog is a good neighbor.

Housetraining Problems

Inappropriate indoor elimination is a smelly, messy problem. It's a problem with which you may not being willing to live. Before reacting by relocating your dog to an outdoor doghouse (not a place for any dog to live), analyze the situation. Did you miss a signal that he needed to go out? Were you away from home so long that he couldn't hold it anymore? These issues aren't problems with housetraining, they are problems generated by you. It's unfair and unreasonable to expect your dog to wait indefinite amounts of time to be let out to his potty area. So, clean up your mess and move on.

On the other hand, your adopted dog may never have been properly housetrained in his former home or in the shelter. If this is the case, start housetraining from the beginning, as you would with a puppy, using a crate and a schedule.

If your dog suddenly begins urinating or defecating in inappropriate areas, make sure the problem is not physical before you decide how to approach the issue behaviorally.

Finding a Pet Behaviorist

Does your dog need the help of a pet behaviorist? Does he have a problem that your training efforts can't resolve? Has his behavior suddenly changed for the worse or increased in severity?

Start with a veterinary exam first. As much as 20 percent of abnormal or problem behaviors can be caused by a medical condition. Once this is ruled out, ask your veterinarian for a referral.

Behaviorists have an education in psychology and are trained to understand pack behavior and canine body language and communication. A few veterinarians are also certified as behaviorists, and you may have access to one if you live near a veterinary college.

If you look for a behavior specialist on your own, make sure that she is certified by either the Animal Behavior Society (ABS) or the International Association of Behavior Consultants (IABC). The IABC website, www.iabc.org, lists practicing members.

If you ask for help from a trainer who is not certified, make certain she is very knowledgeable and has the experience necessary to help.

If your dog has been reliable about housetraining in the past but suddenly starts eliminating indoors, he may be ill. Take him to the vet for an exam, and bring a urine or stool sample. The problem could be caused by a bladder or intestinal infection, the side effect of a medicine, or the result of a change in diet, or it could be an early symptom of a disease. Elderly dogs can become incontinent as their bodies age. Follow your vet's treatment plan and provide your dog with more frequent trips outdoors.

Sometimes major changes in your household or routine may upset your dog or his schedule. For example, adding a new pet may elicit a need in your dog to mark his territory. Or your dog's regular potty times may be affected by your new job or activity away from home. Supervised socialization, reassurance, time, and some help from a neighbor or pet sitter can help solve these particular problems.

Emotional issues, such as fear or stress, can also cause involuntary emptying of the bladder. Fearful dogs, for example, may urinate if a loud noise frightens them. Dogs who've been frightened by particular people sometimes develop a urine-dribbling behavior when greeting them, which means they are acknowledging them as pack leader. If this occurs with you and

SENIOR DOG TIP

Old Dogs, New Tricks

If you adopt your mix as an adult or senior, he may come with behaviors you can't accept in your home. Don't punish him. Try to understand why he acts the way he does. Then put a step-by-step plan in place to retrain him.

Most likely, your new dog will be so happy to have a good home that he'll be anxious to please you. Start by showing and telling him what you want. Interrupt inappropriate behavior and substitute it with an appropriate alternative. Associate short commands with the desired behavior; a command consisting of a single syllable is often easier for a dog to learn than a longer one. For best results, keep training sessions short and end them on a positive note.

You can also take your dog to obedience classes and work with him at home. A dog with a job develops confidence and often is eager to learn—or relearn—new manners.

your dog, clean up the piddle without reacting. When coming home, don't get overly excited when greeting your dog. Wait for him to come to you and calmly pat him. Eventually, most dogs stop urinating submissively.

When housetraining for any inappropriate elimination, go back to the beginning and start over. Allow time for your dog to adapt, heal, or learn. Stay positive; although inconvenient, this problem usually resolves itself over time.

Jumping Up

A dog jumps up so that he can reach a level where he can greet people by smelling or licking their faces. With a large dog, this behavior can be hazardous because you or a visitor could get knocked down. Even a small dog's jumping up may cause you to trip over him. Less hazardous but also a problem, your skin could be scratched or your clothing could be damaged by the dog's toenails.

Sedate dogs (Basset) may be discouraged from jumping up by simply ignoring the behavior. Turn your back to your dog as soon as he starts jumping. When he doesn't get the response he wants, he'll stop. But this method won't work with persistent or energetic mixes.

In most cases, you can stop jumping up by interrupting the behavior. Never knee a dog in the chest. Instead, put your arm out, hand open, palm outward, between you and your dog. Say "off, no jump." Or give the sit and stay command. When your dog keeps all four feet on the floor, praise and greet him. Tiny dogs can be taught not

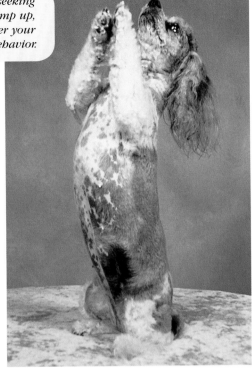

Because most dogs are seeking attention when they jump up, withholding attention whenever your pet does so will discourage the behavior.

to jump up by being placed back onto the floor.

What if you like your dog's enthusiastic greeting and don't want him to stop? It may confuse him if he's only allowed to jump on you only at certain times. Be certain you want this behavior, then train your dog to wait to jump and greet until you give a command to do so.

Separation Anxiety

Separation anxiety occurs when your dog becomes extremely stressed whenever you're away from him. Most dogs learn to be comfortable while you're gone, but a dog who's excessively dependent on you cannot cope and suffers when he's alone.

Dogs who are shy, fearful, overly protective, or don't like to play by themselves may be more prone to developing separation anxiety. If your mix is a rescue, he may come with emotional baggage that makes him anxious if you're out of sight.

Signs that your dog suffers from separation anxiety include panting, pacing, drooling, whining, and nonstop barking or howling. Some dogs may vomit, urinate, or defecate. Seriously anxious dogs often engage in destructive behaviors like chewing through doors or digging up flooring. Extreme cases

may self-mutilate or stop eating.

Try to prevent the behavior first. Don't exhibit emotional neediness yourself, around, or toward your dog. Have different family members feed and walk him. Desensitize your dog to departures by practicing very short trips with no fuss. Some dogs do better if you're able to add another pet to the household for company.

However, if your dog is destroying your home, disturbing the neighbors, or making himself physically ill, check with a behaviorist and your vet. There are therapies and medications that can help.

Chapter 8

Stepping Out

You like to spend time with your dog, having fun and enjoying each other's company. If you get him used to traveling, you can take your mix with you on errands or vacation. And, with some dedicated training, the two of you can recreate together, competing in dog sports or participating in other activities.

Traveling With Your Dog

Most dogs love riding in the car. Say the word "ride" and your dog will probably beat you to the door. But don't assume he's ready to go any place any time. Get him used to travel, and plan ahead for vacations before you get him and go.

Also decide whether your trip is suitable for a dog. Business or adventure trips or vacations where he'll be alone all day may not be best for your canine companion. But if you spend your time hanging out, hiking, or swimming in a calm setting, your dog will probably enjoy your trip as much as you do.

Travel by Car

Get your dog accustomed to travel in the car by taking him on short trips, like to the park for a walk. Take him with you when you run errands. Try a day-long outing such as a picnic and hike. Next take him for an overnight stay.

For his safety, always confine your dog to a crate while he's riding in your vehicle. Place the crate where it sits securely, without sliding or tipping over. Seatbelt-type safety harnesses are

If you decide to travel with your dog, you'll need to make some basic preparations for his travel needs and safety.

also available, as are lift-seats for smaller mixes.

Make sure your dog's ID is current. Use a secondary tag that shows your cell phone number and the number of the hotel or rental where you'll be staying. Carry his picture in your wallet in case he gets away from you while you're vacationing.

Allow one to two hours after feeding and drinking before putting your dog into the car, but try to maintain his normal schedule. While on the road, stop every two or three hours for a potty break and quick drink of water. Even on long travel days, make time for exercising your dog. A tired dog will be a quiet dog and a good hotel guest at night.

During any trip, keep your dog's safety and comfort in mind. Never leave him in the car during hot weather. Even in cooler temperatures, he'll be safest if he's not left alone. Place him into his crate if you have to leave him in your accommodations. This keeps him from getting away or into trouble. Plan activities that you and your dog can enjoy together during the vacation.

Travel by Air

Flying with pets can be complicated these days. Security regulations and reduced flights directly impact your dog's air travel. Plan as far ahead as possible. Try to book a direct flight and only during temperate weather.

If your mix is small, he may be able to fly in the cabin with you as carry-on, but there is a limit to how many dogs are permitted on each flight. You'll

SENIOR DOG TIP

Traveling With Your Senior Dog

If your dog loved to travel when he was younger, he'll probably want to continue to accompany you when he's older too. Stop more often for potty breaks and to give him a chance to stretch stiff joints. He may need to drink or eat smaller amounts but receive them more often. And he may no longer be able to get around as easily as he used to, so make sure he can comfortably keep up with planned activities.

Older dogs whose health is declining, who now stress more easily or suffer from senility, may be better off staying behind. Try to keep your senior at home or in a familiar environment with a pet sitter. On the road or at home, surround your dog with his personal items while you're gone to make him feel more secure.

need extra time to go through security with your dog as well.

Larger dogs have to fly in cargo. Choose an airline that provides pressurized, temperature-controlled space that is lit. Research the airline's

Packing for Your Dog

To make travel comfortable for your dog, prepare a travel bag for him. Pack whatever he'll need to maintain his usual routine, along with other away-from-home essentials. Include:

- food, bowls, bottled water, medications, prepand storage items
- leash, treats, toys, crate, and crate pad
- paper towels, plastic bags for cleanup, spray carpet cleaner, rinseless shampoo
- dog brush, lint brush (for removing hair from furniture and car)
- identification, photo, health records

record of pet flight safety and book the one that can take the best care of your dog.

You'll need a veterinary health certificate that's been issued within ten days of your departure date. Pick a sturdy but ventilated crate for your dog (most air crates are hard plastic or wood). Line it with absorbent pads and soft bedding. Securely attach and partially fill water and food bowls, if the airline permits them. Label his crate with caution signs that read "Live Animal" and "This End Up." Have identification information written on the crate as well.

Some dogs may need to be sedated to fly. Ask your veterinarian for a mild tranquilizer if necessary. Arrive at the airport with sufficient time to get your dog checked into the cargo area. Ask to be notified when he has been loaded onto the plane—and don't leave without him! Supervise his deplaning as well, if possible.

Accommodations

Don't make reservations for your trip and just expect your dog to be welcome wherever you go. Check websites for your lodging and other places of interest you plan to visit to see what their pet permission policies are, or ask when making reservations. Also find out whether there is a limit to the size or number of dogs you can bring and whether there's a pet security deposit. If you use a travel agency, give them your dog's size information and have them reserve accommodations that accept pets.

To satisfy pet-loving customers, many hotel chains and vacation rentals are expanding their policies to permit pets. However, an equal number of locales, such as parks, exclude pets as visitors. Before you leash your dog and take him with you, verify that he's allowed.

Once at your destination, make sure your dog is a well-behaved guest. Don't tie him outside while you're away or leave him alone if he barks. Teach him to be quiet when he hears other guests, especially at night. Clean up any hair that he leaves on the furnishings and clean up after him outdoors. Respecting pet policies helps ensure that your dog, and other pets, will be welcome in the future.

Activities With Your Dog

If walks and fetch aren't enough doggy fun time for you and your dog, check out the numerous organized activities in which you both can participate. Although some dog sports are governed by organizations that accept only registered purebred entries, there are just as many groups that allow dogs of any mix. For example, the American Kennel Club (AKC) has a program for mixed-breed dogs called the AKC Canine Partners Listing Benefits. For a fee, you can enroll your mix and receive special listing benefits and an AKC number for competition eligibility in mixed-breed classes at stand-alone agility, obedience, and rally events. For instructions on how to apply, go to www.akc.org/mixedbreeds/listing_benefits.cfm.

Organized dog sports require that you and your dog work as a team and that your dog is trained to obey basic commands. Developing skills for competition requires dedication and time for training. But the biggest goal is to have fun with your dog.

Whether working in obedience or competing in other activities, working regularly with your dog will strengthen the bond between you, direct his energy in a positive way, and help keep him fit and trim.

When dogs are given an adequate amount of recreation time, they are healthier, happier, and better behaved.

Agility

If your mix is active, athletic, and loves to jump, agility may be right up his alley. In agility, owners direct their dogs through obstacle courses as quickly and correctly as possible. Obstacles include tunnels, jumps set to your dog's height group, weaves, teeters, A-frames, and more.

Dogs earn titles by winning their height and skill division, advancing to greater titles with each class. Events sponsored by the North American Dog Agility Council (NADAC), www.nadac.com, and the United States Dog Agility Association (USDAA), www.usdaa.com, are open to mixed-breed dogs.

Canine Disc

If your dog loves to snatch a disc from the air, he may be a candidate for canine disc competition. Competitions are held throughout the year in various locations around the country. Dogs and owners compete for best freestyle routine (tricks and moves while catching) and longest distance caught.

Organizations sponsoring events include the International Disc Dog Handlers Association, Flying Disc Dog Organization, US Disc Dog Nationals, the UFO World Cup Series of Frisbee, and Skyhoundz World Canine Disc Championship.

Canine Freestyle

Canine freestyle events are demonstrations or competitions during which teams of owners and dogs "dance" a routine to music. The routines are based on obedience commands modified to fit the flow of the music. Participants, both human and dog, wear costumes that match the theme of their song and are judged on style and skill.

A variety of medals are awarded at each competition, and titles are earned based on awards received. Categories for on and off leash, heeling to music, and dance are offered at events. Competitions are open to all dogs through the World Freestyle Canine Organization, www.worldcaninefreestyle.org.

Earthdog

An earthdog is a dog who "goes to ground" to catch his prey. This includes terrier-type dogs (Schnauzer, Scottie,

Dachshund) who burrow or dig to get to rodents or rabbits. Earthdog trials allow your terrier mix to use his natural inclinations to earn titles while having fun.

In competition, tunnels are created for the dogs to go to ground. At the end of the tunnel maze is a cage of one or two rats. (The rats have food and water, are screened so they can't see the dog, and are never caught or touched by the dogs competing.) Dogs earn titles based on the difficulty of the tunnels. Terrier mixes are permitted to compete through the American Working Terrier Association, www.dirt-dog.com/awta.

Flyball

For a mix that loves to catch a ball, run, and jump, flyball may be fun. Teams of four dogs run relays, jumping over hurdles to release a ball, catch it, and return over the jumps to their owner. The fastest team wins. Individual dogs can earn titles for ever-increasing accomplishments.

To get started in flyball, your dog should be obedience trained and familiar with some agility training. Visit www.flyball.org for information on the sport and competitions offered through the North American Flyball Association.

Obedience

Like certain purebreds, many types of mixes excel in obedience work. If you'd like to earn obedience titles with

FAMILY-FRIENDLY TIP

Kids and Doggy Activities

A great way to bring your child and mix together is to participate in some type of organized activity together. This will help them form a close bond and provides a lasting connection between dog and child.

your mix, check out the United Kennel Club at www.ukcdogs.com or the Australian Shepherd Club of America at www.asca.org. Although you must be registered as a member with these groups to compete, they do permit mixed breeds. Most American Kennel Club obedience competitions are open only to registered purebreds, but your mix can compete in mixed-breed classes if you sign up for the AKC's Canine Partners Listing Benefits.

Obedience titles are earned by accurately completing a series of directed, formal commands in multiple events. There are levels of titles, with each level requiring more difficult responses and greater accuracy. The American Mixed Breed Obedience Registration (AMBOR), www.ambor.us, tracks these titles.

If you like doing obedience with your dog but don't want to compete on a formal scale, join a local obedience club and participate in their smaller but equally fun events. An obedience trained dog is always an asset.

Rally-O

Rally-o is a more casual, fun version of obedience, combined with a bit of agility. The Association of Pet Dog Trainers (APDT) allows mixed breeds to compete and earn titles. Again, the AKC also offers rally-o in which your dog may participate if he qualifies for an ILP.

This sport is popular, so training classes for rally-o and competitive events fill quickly. Before beginning, your dog should have basic obedience training and possibly experience with agility. For more information see www.apdt.com/po/rally/about.aspx; AMBOR also records agility titles.

Tracking

Does your mix love to sniff? If he's part scenthound, tracking provides him an opportunity to use his nose. Tracking competitions involve creating a scent trail that your dog must follow as directly as possible to the end, where he finds the scent object.

Start tracking training at home by teaching your dog to find hidden treats. Research the internet, or your local obedience clubs, for groups in your area that sponsor classes where your dog can learn to track outdoors. For serious tracking enthusiasts, see about connecting with a regional Search and Rescue group, where you and your dog can help find lost or injured people.

Therapy Dog

Well-behaved, sociable mixes of any kind are welcome as therapy dogs. Therapy dogs provide a service of compassion by bringing furry smiles to nursing homes, orphanages, and other residential facilities. The residents and patients get to pet and hold your dog, or your dog can entertain them with tricks.

Before beginning therapy dog visits, your dog must pass a test that demonstrates he is suitable for therapy work and is familiar with basic obedience. This test includes correct

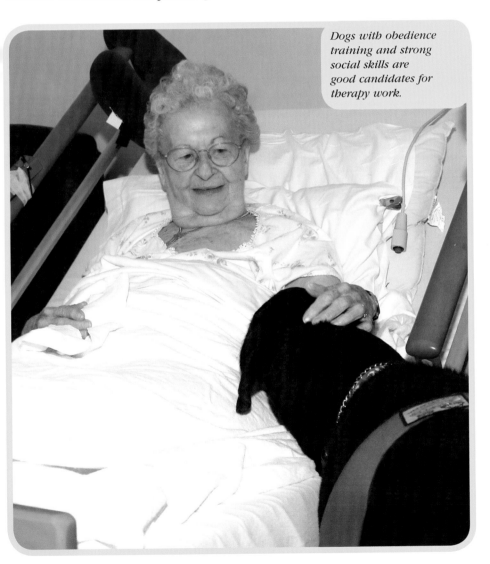

Dogs with obedience training and strong social skills are good candidates for therapy work.

Dog Sports Safety

If you plan to engage in athletic activities or competitive events with your dog, ensure his well-being and safety by doing the following:

- Have a vet examine your dog before beginning any new athletic activity.
- Set a reasonable activity/training schedule, work slowly, and build up to full activity levels gradually.
- If your dog quits or wants to lie down, stop the activity.
- Don't let your dog get overheated; make sure he has plenty of water to stay properly hydrated. Keep him shaded in hot weather, and prevent frostbite in cold weather.
- Always use an appropriate collar, lead, and other equipment; don't improvise.
- Don't jump your dog until he's 18 months old, particularly if he's a large or giant dog, because it may cause damage to growing bones and still-fragile joints.
- Always keep a constant eye on your dog, and avoid dangerous situations.

responses to "sit," "down," and "stay" commands, interactions with strangers, and calm reaction to loud noises. When on a therapy visit, your dog should be clean and healthy.

To find a test date in your area, and information on how to get started, contact Therapy Dogs International, Inc. At www.tdi-dog.org or the Delta Society at www.deltasociety.org. You may also be qualified to help with more extensive therapy assistance programs, such as reading, rehabilitation, or psychotherapy if you have the required education and training.

Other Activities

More dog sports in which you can participate include draft carting (pulling a decorated small wagon), dock jumping (how far your water-type mix can dive, then swim and retrieve), lure coursing (chasing after a moving object tracked by sight), herding instinct tests, sledding, retriever instinct trials, and weight pulling. Train on your own or search for clubs and organizations where you and your dog can compete.

The Mixed Breed Dog Clubs of America (MBDCA) has shows and offers titles for members and their nonpurebred dogs in obedience, rally, lure coursing, and tracking; visit mbdca.tripod.com for information. They also offer conformation events—an activity normally reserved for exceptional purebreds only—for well-proportioned, healthy, athletic, even-tempered, spayed or neutered mixed-breed dogs who are a beauty to behold.

Resources

Associations and Organizations

Breed Clubs

American Canine Hybrid Club
10509 S & G Circle
Harvey, AR 72841
Telephone: (479) 299-4415
E-mail: ach@achclub.com
www.achclub.com

Crossbreed & Mongrel Club
Welton Road
Nettleham, Lincoln
LN2 2LU
United Kingdom
Telephone: 01522 751576
E-mail: chairperson@crossbreed-and-mongrel-club.org.uk
www.crossbreed-and-mongrel-club.org.uk

Mixed Breed Dog Clubs of America
13884 State Route 104
Lucasville, OH 45648-8586
Telephone: (740) 259-3941
E-mail: libi-lew@juno.com
www.mbdca.org

North American Mixed Breed Registry
RR#2 - 8649 Appleby Line
Campbellville, Ontario
Canada L0P 1B0
E-mail: info@nambr.cardoso.ca
www.nambr.cardoso.ca/contact.php

Pet Sitters

National Association of Professional Pet Sitters
15000 Commerce Parkway, Suite C
Mt. Laurel, NJ 08054
Telephone: (856) 439-0324
Fax: (856) 439-0525
E-mail: napps@ahint.com
www.petsitters.org

Pet Sitters International
201 East King Street
King, NC 27021-9161
Telephone: (336) 983-9222
Fax: (336) 983-5266
E-mail: info@petsit.com
www.petsit.com

Rescue Organizations and Animal Welfare Groups

American Humane Association
63 Inverness Drive East
Englewood, CO 80112
Telephone: (303) 792-9900
Fax: 792-5333
www.americanhumane.org

American Society for the Prevention of Cruelty to Animals
424 E. 92nd Street
New York, NY 10128
Telephone: (212) 876-7700
www.aspca.org

Royal Society for the Prevention of
Cruelty to Animals
Telephone: 0870 3335 999
Fax: 0870 7530 284
www.rspca.org.uk

The Humane Society of the United
States
2100 L Street, NW
Washington, DC 20037
Telephone: (202) 452-1100
www.hsus.org

Therapy
Delta Society
875 124th Ave. NE, Suite 101
Bellevue, WA 98005
Telephone: (425) 226-7357
Fax: (425) 235-1076
E-mail: info@deltasociety.org
www.deltasociety.org

Therapy Dogs Incorporated
P.O. Box 20227
Cheyenne, WY 82003
Telephone: (877) 843-7364
E-mail: therapydogsinc@qwestoffice.net
www.therapydogs.com

Therapy Dogs International (TDI)
88 Bartley Road
Flanders, NJ 07836
Telephone: (973) 252-9800
Fax: (973) 252-7171
E-mail: tdi@gti.net
www.tdi-dog.org

Training
Association of Pet Dog Trainers
150 Executive Center Drive, Box 35
Greenville, SC 29615
Telephone: (800) PET-DOGS
Fax: (864) 331-0767
E-mail: information@apdt.com
www.apdt.com

National Association of Dog Obedience
Instructors
PMB 369
729 Grapevine Hwy.
Hurst, TX 76054
www.nadoi.org

Veterinary and Health Resources
Academy of Veterinary Homeopathy
American Academy of Veterinary
Acupuncture
100 Roscommon Drive, Suite 320
Middletown, CT 06457
Telephone: (860) 635-6300
Fax: (860) 635-6400
E-mail: office@aava.org
www.aava.org

American Animal Hospital Association
P.O. Box 150899
Denver, CO 80215-0899
Telephone: (303) 986-2800
Fax: (303) 986-1700
E-mail: info@aahanet.org
www.aahanet.org/index.cfm

American College of Veterinary Internal Medicine

1997 Wadsworth Blvd., Suite A
Lakewood, CO 80214-5293
Telephone: (800) 245-9081
Fax: (303) 231-0880
E-mail: ACVIM@ACVIM.org

www.acvim.org

American College of Veterinary Ophthalmologists

P.O. Box 1311
Meridian, ID 83860
Telephone: (208) 466-7624
Fax: (208) 466-7693
E-mail: office@acvo.com
www.acvo.com

American Holistic Veterinary Medical Association

2218 Old Emmorton Road
Bel Air, MD 21015
Telephone: (410) 569-0795
Fax: (410) 569-2346
E-mail: office@ahvma.org
www.ahvma.org

American Veterinary Medical Association

1931 North Meacham Road, Suite 100
Schaumburg, IL 60173
Telephone: (847) 925-8070
Fax: (847) 925-1329
E-mail: avmainfo@avma.org
www.avma.org

ASPCA Animal Poison Control Center
1717 South Philo Road, Suite 36
Urbana, IL 61802
Telephone: (888) 426-4435
www.aspca.org/pet-care/poison-control/

British Veterinary Association
7 Mansfield Street
London
W1G 9NQ
United Kingdom
Telephone: 020 7636 6541
Fax: 020 7436 2970
E-mail: bvahq@bva.co.uk
www.bva.co.uk

Canine Eye Registration Foundation
VMDB/CERF
1248 Lynn Hall
625 Harrison St.
Purdue University
West Lafayette, IN 47907-2026
Telephone: (765) 494-8179
E-mail: CERF@vmbd.org
www.vmdb.org

Orthopedic Foundation for Animals
2300 NE Nifong Blvd.
Columbus, MI 65201
Telephone: (573) 442-0418
Fax: (573) 875-5073
E-mail: ofa@offa.org
www.offa.org

Index

Note: **Boldfaced** numbers indicate illustrations.

110

Index

About the Author

Lexiann Grant is an internationally published, award-winning pet writer and photographer who has raised, trained, shown, written, and spoken about dogs and cats for many years. She is a professional member of the Dog Writers Association of America and has been a recipient of the Maxwell Medallion eight times. Lexiann works full-time in her home office, where much of her time is spent observing the pets with whom she lives. She cohabits with three dogs, six cats, and four bicycles.

Photo Credits